BLOOD AND GRANITE

BLOOD AND GRANITE

TRUE CRIME FROM ABERDEEN

NORMAN ADAMS

BLACK & WHITE PUBLISHING

First published 2003
by Black & White Publishing Ltd
99 Giles Street, Edinburgh EH6 6BZ

ISBN 1 902927 64 8

Printed and bound by Creative Print and Design

CONTENTS

ACKNOWLEDGEMENTS

Many people have helped in my search for murder and mystery in Aberdeen in the twentieth century and I am indebted to all of them. I wish to thank ex-Detective Superintendent Harry Halcrow, the former head of Aberdeen CID, who generously shared some of his experiences during his time with the force, which he joined in 1939. I am also grateful to other former policemen for their assistance. These include: Jim McLeod, who rose through the ranks to retire as boss of Grampian Police CID in 1988; Hamish Irvine, who wrote the first official history of Grampian Police while a serving officer; and Raymond Mack, Grampian Police Welfare Officer. Journalists who provided me with the backgrounds to several cases include: Graeme Smith, *The Herald*'s man in Aberdeen; Ken Banks of Newsline Scotland Press Agency in Aberdeen; Adam Borthwick, who was Northern News Editor of the *Scottish Daily Express*; Ione Campsie, *Sunday Post*, Aberdeen; Ron Paton, London Editor, D C Thomson & Co. Ltd.; Ron Ferrier, former Assistant Editor of Aberdeen's *Evening Express*; and Gordon Argo, retired Aberdeen journalist.

My sincere thanks are also due to Ian Watson, Head of Rights and Information, SMG Publishing, for allowing me to use material from the *Glasgow Herald*, subsequently *The Herald*. Donald Martin, Editor of Aberdeen's *Evening Express*, David Knight, Assistant Editor, *Press and Journal* and David Hamilton, Executive Editor, *Scottish Daily Express*, also gave me permission to use information from their files.

I must also thank Mr Hamilton and The Mitchell Library, Glasgow, for allowing the use of the 'Phantom' photograph and Murray Foote, Deputy Editor, *Daily Record*, for his help. I am grateful to Aberdeen Journals Ltd, their head librarian Duncan Smith, colleague Bob Stewart and printer Bruce Irvine for providing illustrations and information. Credit also goes to Tony Murray of SMG Picture Library, Glasgow, to my son, Norman G Adams and to William Gloyer who gave me permission to use the Betty Hadden search picture which was taken by his late father, Marshall H Gloyer.

Special thanks also go to J Geddes Wood, founder of Scotpix, Aberdeen, for providing a portfolio of graphic shots, many of which have never before been published.

I am also grateful to Rev. John Dickson, Banchory, and William Bruce, Aberdeen, for sharing their memories and to author Alanna Knight for her support. Denise Marshall of Grampian Police Media Services and the Scottish Prison Services were also most helpful. My thanks are also due to Daphne Plowman, editor of *The PSI Report*, Dr Peter McCue, David M Burnside, Robbie Glen, Bob McGregor and my editors, Ivor Norman and Patricia Marshall.

Final thanks go to the staff at Aberdeen Central Library (Reference and Local Studies) and the General Services Department and the Archives and Special Collections at the Mitchell Library for dealing with my numerous inquiries.

INTRODUCTION

Aberdeen, City of Blood and Granite. The capital of north-east Scotland bears no such stigma but it had its share of notable killings in the twentieth century. It's known world-wide as Oil Boom City or City for All Seasons and, oh, yes, Britain in Bloom City – although it has won the trophy so many times that people have lost count. But, like any other city of its size, Aberdeen has its dark side and this book chronicles murder and mystery in the city during the last century.

So, first, an intriguing question – can a neighbourhood become haunted by crime? By a strange twist of fate, six brutal twentieth-century slayings are associated with the old road to Gallow Hill. In the early Middle Ages, the Justice or Thieves' Port, on the east side of the Castlegate, was the gateway to Justice Street, which led to 'Heiding' or Heading Hill. Here, criminals were 'heidit' either with a two-handed sword or by means of 'The Maiden', a type of primitive guillotine. A deep grassy cleft, separating Heading Hill and Castlehill, was the place where witches were strangled and then burned. Today, traffic fumes have replaced the stench of burning flesh.

In later times, Justice Street was the start of the circuitous journey to Gallow Hill (now part of Erroll Street and Trinity Cemetery), reached by way of present-day Park Street over the 'Thieves' Brig'. The old brig no longer exists. It spanned the old Powcreek Burn the bed of which was used as part of the Aberdeen–Port Elphinstone canal. A single-track freight railway line later followed its route and this is still in use today. The public road branched right to the Links, while the gallows road forked left into present-day Urquhart Place. It joined on to what is now Urquhart Road, then turned sharply north and headed uphill by Urquhart Lane, to its final destination at Gallow Hill where, in the eighteenth century, culprits were hanged and their corpses either encased in a suit of iron or surrendered to the anatomists.

In close proximity to this haunted highway, some of the city's most infamous crimes took place. Innocent blood was spilt at both ends of the old road to the gibbet, beginning with the fatal stabbing of two butchers in the Saltoun Arms pub in 1901 – our first murders in this book – and ending with a shotgun murder forty-years ago which resulted in the perpetrator, Harry Burnett, becoming the last man to hang in Scotland. Three months after Burnett was executed at Craiginches Prison in Aberdeen, the body of a boy, who had been missing for four months, was exhumed from the floor of a greenhouse on Heading Hill. The murder of a six-year-old Woodside girl almost three years earlier was finally solved and the killer of both children was put away.

Opposite the north end of Urquhart Place, where the old gallows road emerged, stands No. 61 Urquhart Road. In April 1934, Jeannie Donald, an ordinary Aberdeen housewife murdered her neighbours' daughter. Eight-year-old Helen Priestly's body was later found in a sack dumped in the common lobby. Donald's decision not to give evidence has led to a great deal of theory and speculation to this day. By a grim coincidence, Helen's mother, broke the news of their daughter's disappearance to her husband at the Saltoun Arms, where he was doing painting work. Jeannie Donald was reprieved, otherwise she might have been executed by the Pierrepoints. These two hangmen were blood relatives – uncle and nephew. Burnett, on the other hand, was hanged by Harry Allen, Britain's last surviving hangman, who died in 1992, at the age of eighty. Allen's wax effigy was displayed in Madame Tussaud's Chamber of Horrors in the 1960s.

INTRODUCTION

Everyone loves a good mystery and the murder of Betty Hadden, the teenager the press dubbed the 'waterfront waif', continues to baffle people – even although almost sixty years have elapsed since she died. The mystery began when the tide in the navigation channel cast up her severed arm – but, despite intensive and exhaustive investigation, there was only silence. The file on Hadden isn't the only one marked 'unsolved'. Two major murders – those of the brilliant Aberdeen University scientist, Dr Brenda Page, and the taxi driver, George Murdoch – share that common factor with the Hadden mystery. Despite hours of hard slog by detectives and uniformed officers, no physical evidence links the victims to their attackers. During the Murdoch inquiry, police mounted a surprise operation before a big football match at Aberdeen's ground in an effort to snare his killer.

But 'cold cases' are never closed. In recent years, Aberdeen forensic scientists have carried out the latest DNA techniques on certain pieces of evidence and some key witnesses have been re-interviewed. DNA (deoxyribonucleic acid) is present in living cells and contains the genetic code that makes each person unique. One day, the use of DNA fingerprinting might bring one of these killers to justice.

Police officers are a special breed – they have to be considering the abject misery and tragedy they have to deal with in the wake of violent crime. It is a job that, by its very nature, entails a certain compassionate detachment. But child murder – that most heinous of crimes – tests the mettle of even the most hardened member of the force. It may come as a surprise to learn that the callous murder of a baby in the mid 1950s made modern Scottish legal history – a conviction without a body. Only three subsequent Scottish murder trials have gone ahead without a body.

East End, West End – as we'll see, a sought-after postcode is no protection against vicious crime. A killer can strike at anytime, anywhere. The city's most heart-rending child murders took place at different ends of the social spectrum. Tenement flats, pubs and

11

dark streets are not the only places defiled by wrongful death. The lofty steeple of St Mary's Cathedral marks the spot of the brutal killing of Sister Josie, a much-loved nun. The crime horrified the city but her murder also brought out the goodness and goodwill of the its citizens.

A knife is the most frequently used murder weapon in Scotland. Attacks with knives, scissors and a broken wine bottle are the cause of many of the deaths mentioned in this book but other victims were shot, bludgeoned or strangled and one, a policeman, was dragged to his death by a motor car. Jealousy, hate, greed, rage and lust are just some of the things that turned people into killers. Other killings were fuelled by alcohol or drugs. Those who broke the Sixth Commandment are now dead or free, after serving their sentences, or still locked up. But a few, whose identities are a mystery, may still be walking our streets.

Sensitivity towards the feelings of friends and families of the victims of some of Aberdeen's most recent murders dictates that these are not covered here.

1

CUTTING EDGE

1901

The stench of blood hung in the air as butchers, in greasy aprons, toiled all day and late into the night at the Wales Street slaughter-house in the East End of the city. On the night of 9 January 1901, three workmates walked the short distance to the Saltoun Arms public house on the corner of Park Street, which follows the line of the road to the gallows. About 10.30 p.m., James Harrow (33), William Tastard (44) and young John (known as 'Jeek') Rae entered the doorway, with its polished granite pillars and gold-lettered sign, facing South Constitution Street. Gaslight shimmered on the etched mirrors, the polished horseshoe- shaped counter and the array of glass tumblers and bottles neatly stacked on the gantry shelves. A fire glowed in the grate. A few customers stood at the bar or relaxed in the seats running round the walls on the Frederick Street and Park Street sides of the premises. The Saltoun, named after the family of Saltoun of Cairnbulg, was a modern and reputable establishment owned by Cornelius Mearns. When the three butchers came into the pub, Mearns was out at the stable at the back. There was little hint of the terrible crime that was to follow within the next few minutes.

Harrow, a surly and silent individual, nursed a grievance. The barman and customers would later say that the three butchers had not exchanged angry words but that Harrow had let his ill-feeling towards Tastard be known. Harrow was carrying a butcher's knife, wrapped in newspaper, and, in the heat of the moment, he produced the formidable weapon. 'Take that!' he cried as he struck out at Tastard. The burly, moustachioed Harrow lunged at his hapless victim, who tried to dodge the gleaming blade. But Tastard was stabbed twice – in the neck and in the chest. The wound in his neck was ghastly. As he had ducked, the blade gashed his nape and, according to eye-witnesses, almost severed the spinal cord. The second wound penetrated his chest and cut his heart in two. Tastard dropped dead on the spot.

A thrill of horror gripped witnesses. David Ewing (29), who also worked as a butcher, had been drinking close by and he challenged Harrow, asking him if he realised what he had done. The dripping blade, resembling some obscene tongue, was Harrow's response. He promptly used it to stab his second victim in the chest. Ewing sank to the floor in a pool of his own blood. Then, as if possessed by a devil, Harrow went his after his other drinking companion, 'Jeek' Rae. But, as panic erupted, the quick-witted Rae threw his jacket at Harrow and bolted. The killer gave chase but melted into the night as a policeman blew his whistle and shouted, 'Murder!'

The news of the murder was carried to the Central Police Office in Lodge Walk by a constable. Several bobbies were sent to the blood-spattered Saltoun Arms and they were followed by Chief Constable Thomas Wyness and Superintendent Morren. Inspector Bill Buchan had taken charge of the premises and, by this time, a doctor had been summoned. Dr James Moncur quickly arrived from his surgery in King Street, at the other end of Frederick Street, but there was nothing he could do for Tastard. However, he did dress Davie Ewing's gaping wound.

Chief Constable Wyness told waiting reporters, 'I have seen a few ugly gashes in the course of my forty years' experience but never did I see such a wound on a man who is still alive. Why, you could put your hand in it.' The Chief Constable, a farmer's son from Midmar in Aberdeenshire, was an innovative policeman. He introduced horse transport and cycle patrols to Aberdeen and was unrelenting in his crack-down on back-shop boozing in licensed grocers. He was parodied in a poem, 'The New Dictator', but, by the time of his death at the end of 1902, he had gone a long way to improve and promote the efficiency of the force.

In spite of his fearful wound, Ewing was helped to his feet and taken to the infirmary in Woolmanhill. But what of Harrow? Less than an hour after the attack, he was arrested at 61 Park Street, where he lived with his mother. The arresting officers, Inspectors Buchan and Wilson, found the killer sitting down to supper. On searching the apartment, they found a skinner's knife under a bed. Its blade – six inches long and an inch broad and curved like a scimitar – was clotted with blood and animal hairs adhered to its short handle. At this point, the police believed that they had found the murder weapon. Harrow's mother buried her head in her arms. A huge crowd had already gathered outside the house and constables had to clear a path for Harrow, who was handcuffed to Inspector Buchan and Sergeant Robertson. Harrow was brought to the police headquarters at about 11.45 p.m. to face a very relieved Chief Constable Wyness, who, no doubt, feared that the killer was still at large and that his bloodlust had not yet been slaked.

In the charge room, a sullen and indifferent Harrow, still dressed in his working clothes of greasy jacket and cloth cap, was cautioned by the be-whiskered Wyness in lofty tones, 'Now, my man, you need not say anything unless you care to but I have had you apprehended on a charge of murder and you are to be detained here on that charge.' After confirming his name, age, address and occupation, the accused was searched then locked up in a cell. Eleven witnesses were interviewed at police headquarters and it was 2.30 a.m. before they were allowed home. Before that, they were each asked if they could identify the accused. As the witnesses filed past him, Harrow stood calm and erect and they replied in the affirmative. Harrow gave no sign of recognition.

The morning after the murder, townsfolk awoke to the bold headline in the *Aberdeen Journal*, 'TERRIBLE TRAGEDY IN ABERDEEN', below which were gory details of the events at the Saltoun Arms.

What they did not know was that the police now really did have the murder weapon. It had been found at 2.30 am – too late to catch the newspaper's deadline – on a windowsill of the East End Evangelical Mission in Frederick Street, just round the corner from the pub. The butcher's knife was bloodstained and wrapped round the handle was a piece of paper saturated with blood. Its four inch blade was said to be as 'keen as a lance'. Scribes hot-footed it to the deceased's home at 13 Marischal Street, near the docks. There, they found out that the victim was a bachelor who lived with his aged mother. They also discovered that Mrs Tastard ran a shop in the Shiprow, known to generations of Aberdonians for cooking the tastiest of potted-head.

The family's lives had been blighted by tragedy several times in the past. In under than two years, Mrs Tastard had been widowed and had lost both her daughter and her son-in-law. Her murdered son had supported the dead couple's orphaned sons. Two decades earlier, the Tastard's eldest son, James, had drowned in a bathing accident in the Falls of Feugh at Banchory.

At noon on 10 January, Harrow was escorted by two policemen to the Sheriff Courthouse where he appeared in private before Sheriff Burnet. Shortly before, he had been led from his cell into the courtyard at Lodge Walk where, in the dull light of a lowering winter day, he was photographed by Detective George Gibb. An office stool was placed outside the muster-room window and the accused posed, without a murmur, as Gibb ordered him to sit still and place his hands flat on his knees. Gibb took two shots – a full-face portrait and a profile. In chambers, Harrow was charged with Tastard's murder and with seriously assaulting Ewing to the danger of his life. The officials, who also included Procurator Fiscal Maclennan and the defence solicitor, G M Aitken, were said to have been surprised by Harrow's cool demeanour. Apart from confirming personal details, on the advice of his legal agent, he made no further statement. Harrow then signed the declaration 'without a tremor' before returning to the courtyard separating the police headquarters from the courthouse. He stepped briskly into a horse-drawn 'Black Maria', along with two constables, and was driven to Craiginches Prison, which was built in 1891, on the rocky Craiglug on the south side of the Dee. He was placed in solitary confinement under the close supervision of a warder, who kept watch on the untried prisoner through a window in the cell door in case Harrow attempted suicide or tried a daring escape. During his stint, the duty officer had to clock on periodically so there was little chance of him dozing off.

'The Aberdeen Tragedy', as it was dubbed by the press, eclipsed news of the Boer War, where disease, and not the resourceful enemy, had accounted for thousands of British deaths. In China, the Boxer Rebellion had been snuffed out and Allied peace proposals had been presented to the Manchus. But it was the bloodletting at home that gripped the Aberdonians. One editorial pointed out that, in the past, butchers had had the reputation 'of being like Italians – too ready with the knife in case of a quarrel'. (Ironically, two weeks later, a drunken row between two Italian traders at a house in Justice Street ended in bloodshed when one of them stabbed his friend.) The familiarity with the killing of dumb animals, it added, had the effect on 'some men of low type of blunting the feeling as to the sacredness of human life'. The writer was quick to add that Tastard, a butcher since boyhood, had been a man of the most humane and kindly disposition. Harrow, on the other hand, appeared to have been morose and gloomy and his habits were less steady.

But what had caused Harrow to behave so savagely? What had driven him to murder? His acquaintances, who were few, described how 'Peter', as he was known, enjoyed his own company. He was said to prefer sitting alone in a pub, nursing a 'schooner' of beer, while engrossed in a sporting paper, for he liked to gamble on the horses. He was not a man to be trifled with, it was said. Harrow and his victim were believed to have been on friendly terms. Indeed, a few weeks before the murder, Tastard had invited

Harrow home for dinner. On display in the house was a photograph of the two men taken at work. In it, Tastard was standing arms akimbo and the snout of Harrow's 'Italian cap' cast a shadow over his eyes.

Tastard was a foreman butcher and Harrow, who had worked at the slaughterhouse since his youth, had relied on Tastard and other butchers for regular employment. But, in the months leading up to the crime, Harrow had found himself overlooked. Jobs had been given to other part-time butchers and, because of this, he bore Tastard a grudge. The grudge grew into deep hatred and he was heard to make dire threats against the foreman and 'Jeek' Rae, who had been preferred to him more than once. The threats were treated lightly by Tastard but Rae was a worried man. He warned Tastard's mother but she laughed in his face. Rae feared that Tastard's associates might also be singled out by Harrow.

Butcher Alexander Bannochie, who claimed to be on good terms with Harrow, cast more light on Harrow's motive for murder. Early in the evening of 9 January, Harrow had confided, 'I am to go for Tastard tonight.' Bannochie was not worried at the time but he knew all about his friend's grievance against Tastard and the butchers he would hire in preference to Harrow. Bannochie had been drinking in the Saltoun Arms when Harrow, Tastard and Rae arrived on the fateful night. Sensing trouble, he left. The three men had been working throughout the day and were taking time off for a refreshment before returning to work.

The Saltoun was not their usual howff. They had gone there for one reason – to persuade Harrow to go home, after buying him a dram to placate him. Davie Ewing was to replace him for the rest of the shift. Harrow had probably known he was being replaced by Ewing before he arrived at the pub. Within ten minutes, Tastard was stone dead and Ewing was in a grave condition. From his sickbed, Ewing assured his wife there had been no heated argument with Harrow. Harrow had beckoned to Tastard with a nod of the head, as if to make a remark outwith the hearing of the others. He had then lunged at the unsuspecting foreman. Ewing, who was the father of a ten-year-old daughter, lingered in hospital for four days. The medical men had hoped he would make a recovery but complications arose and he died from 'traumatic delirium and inflammation of the lungs' on the afternoon of 13 January.

That morning, they had buried Tastard amid scenes bordering on the chaotic. A crowd of 40,000 thronged Union Street as the coffin was carried in relays on its mile-long journey from the deceased's home in Marischal Street to Nellfield Cemetery in the West End. (In 1899, the cemetery had been at the centre of a scandal in which lairs were emptied to make room for fresh burials.) Police had to clear a path as the plain black coffin was carried by four young butchers down the stair of No. 13 and into the street. There had been a morbid interest in the question of which mortcloth would be draped over the coffin. Tastard had been prominent in the move to acquire a new funeral pall for the local butchers' society and, if delivered in time, it would make its first appearance at his own funeral. The deceased had been a member of the Court Granite City Ancient Order of Foresters and, in the end, it was their mortcloth that covered the coffin lid. Resting on top were the organisation's silver horn and Tastard's regalia.

In Castle Street and Union Street, thousands impeded the progress of the cortège and dozens of police officers had to force a passage for the slow-moving procession. Men raised their hats in respect, women sobbed and children gawped. At the cemetery, some of the spectators climbed the walls for a better view. Among the mourners were the killer's brother, Bill Harrow, 'Jeek' Rae and Cornelius Mearns of the Saltoun Arms, whose pub did a roaring trade the night after the murders. Ewing's father, also named David, who ran his own butcher's business in the New Market, paid his respects too. He would soon learn of his son's death.

Three days later, the scenes at Davie Ewing's funeral were more orderly and the posse of police had little to do. A large, silent crowd watched as the coffin, borne on the broad shoulders of the dead man's workmates, was carried past the Saltoun Arms Bar in Park Street and along Frederick Street to King Street. The cortège turned north on the long walk to St Peter's Cemetery, with its great iron gates bearing a skull and crossbones and the motto *Non sibi sed cunctis* – 'Not for self but for all'. Mourners included the late Bill Tastard's brother, 'Jeek' Rae and Cornelius Mearns.

Even as they buried Ewing, the defence solicitor was calling on his client at Craiginches Prison. He made no mention to Harrow of Ewing's funeral. The unruffled Harrow had no other visitors but it did not blunt his appetite. The prison menu consisted of milk and porridge for breakfast and supper, with broth, potatoes and bread for lunch. Prisoners of the day would have been able to supplement this meagre fare with a limited supply of liquor and food brought in from the outside by visitors.

After Ewing's funeral, public interest turned to other lurid headlines. George Henry Parker, who had been drummed out of the Royal Marines, had shot two fellow passengers in a railway carriage on the South–Western Line between Southampton and Waterloo. One victim, farmer William Pearson, did not survive and Parker would be hanged for his murder at Wandsworth. Readers of the *Aberdeen Journal* no doubt received a nasty jolt when they scanned the headline 'BOER ATTACK ON ABERDEEN'. But they had nothing to fear. This particular Aberdeen was a South African village and a Boer commando force had been driven off thanks to the gallantry of a few British troops. Closer to home, the Shetland Disaster Fund, which gave financial support to fifteen families who had lost their menfolk in a recent fishing-boat disaster, was growing.

Queen Victoria expressed her deep sympathy and sent a cheque for £20. On 22 January, black bordered columns carried the news of her death. Interest in 'The Aberdeen Tragedy' was diverted but, three days after the Queen's passing and the ascent of King Edward VII, Aberdonians learned from the press that Harrow had been examined by doctors and was unlikely to stand trial because of his insanity. The news came as no surprise to readers of the *Aberdeen Free Press*. In an interview with the paper, Harrow's family said that the accused's brother had been confined to a mental asylum and Harrow himself harboured strange delusions about his workmates, believing Tastard had tried to poison him. Harrow's brother-in-law had taken Harrow on holiday to Edinburgh before the New Year and he had returned in a peaceful, sane frame of mind. But the accused's delusions returned to haunt him, with tragic results.

Harrow was brought to the High Court of Justiciary in Aberdeen on Friday 29 March 1901 to face two counts of murder. At the Sheriff Court Pleading Diet ten days earlier, Harrow had pleaded not guilty and his counsel lodged a special defence that the accused was insane when he committed the murders. The court proceedings were due to start at 10.30 a.m. but, by nine, a huge crowd had already gathered outside the courthouse in Castle Street. A cere-monial guard of honour was mounted at the front door by Gordon Highlanders with fixed bayonets, as police kept the public in check.

At 10.20 a.m., trumpeters, in scarlet coats with gold trim and cocked hats, blew a fanfare as the judge, Lord McLaren, walked along the corridor with a measured tread, preceded by a mace-bearer. By the time the judge took his seat on the bench, the courtroom was packed with representatives of the Town Council, police and the legal profession. Several of the victims' relatives, in mourning dress, occupied seats in the gallery.

After a short prayer, Harrow, followed by a constable, entered the courtroom by a trapdoor from the cells below. He kept his head down, his eyes darting to right and left. Twenty-three witnesses had been summoned to give evidence for the prosecution. There were eleven defence witnesses but, as it turned out, only two of the eleven were called to give evidence. They were both doctors – Professor Matthew Hay and Dr William Reid, medical superintendent at the Aberdeen Royal Asylum – who were asked to describe the accused's state of mind.

Although Tastard and Harrow had been on friendly terms, the doctors said that Harrow laboured under the delusion that Tastard had plotted to kill him. The previous December, while drinking together in a pub close to their workplace, Harrow believed that Tastard had poisoned his whisky. He fell very ill next day – 'a dragging at the heart, restlessness and sleeplessness' – and left for Edinburgh the day after to get out of the way of his suspected assassin. His health improved on his homecoming but next he suspected Tastard of trying to attack him with a knife at work. He had stabbed Tastard in self-defence, he told the doctors.

Professor Hay gave the accused's account of what took place in the Saltoun Arms on the fatal night. Harrow had gone to the pub with Tastard and their workmates for a friendly drink. There were no angry words between them but Harrow claimed, when they had finished their drinks, Tastard had seized him by his coat lapels and told him 'to come away down'. Somehow, the mentally unstable butcher believed he was to be led back to the slaughter-house to be killed. In his pocket was a knife he had used that day to kill sheep. He completely lost his head and stabbed Tastard in a struggle. Ewing had grabbed him and tried to trip him up.

Hay, who had interviewed the accused on several occasions since his arrest, described him as a man of weak mental capacity but added that he had a more remarkable memory than almost any man he had met. 'He could give dates for a long time past, on matters affecting himself but he was most undoubtedly of weak intellect regarding ordinary affairs.' Apart from his delusions and hallucinations regarding Tastard, Ewing and 'Jeek' Rae, Harrow had morbid suspicions and 'hallucinations of hearing' in connection with other workmates. Harrow told Dr Reid that he heard their voices threatening to kill him. When asked about a final interview he had had with Harrow before the court commenced that morning, Dr Reid said the accused was still labouring under various illusions and hallucinations and was of unsound mind and quite irresponsible for his actions. He was incapable of understanding the charge against him and unable to instruct his defence.

Lord McLaren asked, 'You make a distinction between illusions and hallucinations. What is the difference?' and Dr Reid replied, 'To give you an example of a hallucination, I see before me at the present time something that does not exist; that is a hallucination.' He pointed to a gas bracket. 'An illusion would be this: I see the globe of that gas over there. If I misinterpret that for something else, that would be an illusion. In the same way with regard to hearing, I might hear a voice which did not exist. That would be a hallucination of hearing, whereas, if I have heard rain or something of that nature on the roof and I misinterpret that for something else, that would be an illusion of hearing.'

Both doctors agreed that excessive drinking could cause permanent insanity. Harrow's delusions seemed to get worse with excessive drinking. The butchers of Wales Street appeared to have been heavy drinkers. In the course of their long working day, they might each consume about half a bottle of spirits in local pubs, having started at four in the morning.

After the hour-long hearing, Lord McLaren found Harrow insane and ordered him to be detained during the new monarch's pleasure. The *Aberdeen Journal* reported, 'With a bang, the trapdoor closed and the public of Aberdeen had presumably seen the last of the man whose mad crime so much shocked the community.' Harrow was spirited away to Craiginches in a 'Black Maria' and was later confined at Perth Prison in a wing for the mentally disturbed that was described as being 'similar to the fatuous ward of a poorhouse'.

In summing up the event, the paper, ignoring the fact that it had carried a wealth of prejudicial evidence before the case had come to court, complained, 'In this case, everybody seemed to know everything.' While grateful that a charge of double murder was a rare occurrence in Aberdeen, the *Journal* pointed out that there had been no sensational feature, no subtle acts usually associated with a poisoning trial or a deliberately planned and

23

carefully calculated crime such as the Yarmouth tragedy, which had gripped its readers. Eight days before Harrow was sentenced, Herbert John Bennett (22) was hanged at Norwich for the murder of his wife, Mary, whom he had strangled with a boot lace on Yarmouth beach.

The day after Harrow's High Court appearance, two big sporting events took place – the Grand National and the annual England–Scotland football match. No doubt, if fate had been more kind, Harrow, the inveterate gambler, would have been engrossed in a sporting paper in his local pub, tempted by the odds at Aintree and at Crystal Palace.

Harrow was not the first butcher to kill a workmate. On 23 April 1886, William Erskine, nicknamed 'Sparkie' – probably because of his short temper which was frequently fuelled by drinking bouts – stabbed Joe Leith through the heart in a fight at the West Hutcheon Street slaughterhouse. Leith, a well-known long-distance walker, wrestled his opponent to the ground and held him down but then he collapsed and died from loss of blood. It appeared that Leith had been teasing 'Sparkie'. Erskine pled guilty to culpable homicide and was given five years' hard labour.

2

FATAL FOOTSTEPS

1961

Church bells summoned a trickle of worshippers to evening services on the second Sabbath of 1961 in Woodside as a little girl lay dying in a gutter. Her neck bore a horrific wound. June Cruickshank, a sweet-faced six-year-old, had left home a short time before to buy a packet of custard powder in a shop at the corner of Great Northern Road and Pirie's Lane. Kincaid's shop was only 135 yards away from June's home on the middle floor of a council tenement at 7 Printfield Walk. June handed over the sixpence her mother had given her and the female assistant handed back a halfpenny change.

June was well liked by the staff at Kincaid's, where she often bought sweets and 'messages' for her mum. On that evening of Sunday 8 January 1961, June had been wearing a royal blue cardigan, a buff-coloured pullover and a navy blue skirt to keep out the cold, raw air. She also had on boys' ankle socks, in the navy blue and gold colours of Gordon's College, and brown lacing shoes. Her short, fair hair was tied in a light blue ribbon. When June left the shop, it was shortly before 6 p.m. Then she must have met her killer who lured her into a dark, eerie lane – a cul-de-sac on the north-east side of Great Northern Road – where he cut her throat.

June's mum, Mrs Anne Cruickshank, found she was short of something else and sent her son, Brian, aged twelve, to Kincaid's, mentioning that his sister was taking rather a long time. Brian returned with the item but he had seen nothing of his sister. By now, June had apparently found the strength to cross the main road, momentarily deserted of traffic, to collapse in a pool of blood, within sight of the lights of home. A trail of blood led from the cul-de-sac to the spot where she was found, clutching the packet of pudding mixture and with a copper halfpenny under her body.

It was Maureen Higgins (26), on her way to catch a bus to choir practice at St Mary's Cathedral in the city centre, who made the grim discovery. At first she thought the crumpled heap was a dog lying at the side of the road at the Printfield bus terminus. It appeared to be crawling. When she drew closer, the glow of the street lights exposed the full horror. The front of the child's clothing was soaked in blood.

Shipyard worker Robert Munro, who had been visiting his mother in Printfield Walk, was a father-to-be. He too was catching a bus into town with the intention of visiting his wife in the maternity home. June was barely alive when he got to her. He placed a hand on her pale brow and spoke words of comfort. Maureen, a Girl Guide leader, covered the prone body with her coat. Mr Munro waved down a passing motorist and asked him to fetch the police.

It was just at that harrowing moment when Mrs Cruickshank looked out of the window to see if there was any sign of her daughter heading back home. Mr Munro shouted up to her, 'Is it a little girl you are looking for?' When she agreed it was, Mr Munro told her, 'There's a little girl down here.' A distressed Mrs Cruickshank rushed downstairs to her daughter's side. An ambulance was called but June was beyond help. At first, Mrs Cruickshank thought her daughter had been the victim of a road accident. She was not told of how she had died until her taxi-driver husband, David, returned from police headquarters.

Every available policeman and detective turned out as Aberdeen's biggest murder hunt for years began. It was led by Detective Chief Inspector Donald McIntosh, head of Aberdeen CID. Rennie, the police force's ace tracker dog, an Alsatian and the scourge of city burglars, was brought in to search the murder scene. A detachment of firemen turned spotlights on the narrow, dark lane where June had been brutally attacked to allow detectives to search for clues. The area was cordoned off. In Printfield Walk, a wooden door and planks protected the spot where June's body had lain and no vehicles were allowed into the street. Senior detectives set up field headquarters in the corporation cleansing department building next door to the cul-de-sac.

At 10 o'clock that night, Chief Constable Alexander Matheson called a press conference at police headquarters in Lodge Walk. He told reporters, 'We are anxious to find anyone who may have seen a man or a youth in the girl's company or a man or a youth with bloodstained clothing in the vicinity of Printfield Walk or the Fountain area of Woodside.' (The area gets its name from a drinking well that once stood at a road junction.)

News of the shocking murder caused terror in the community. At Woodside Primary School, where June had been a pupil, hundreds of youngsters were allowed out early so that they could get home before daylight failed. Worried mothers collected their children at the gates. 'I'll do my ain messages from now on,' said one mother. The *Press and Journal* reported that parents in Woodside were in the grip of fear.

The police knocked on doors from one end of Great Northern Road to the other. On the morning after the murder, a telephone directory was handed to them. It had been found in a phone booth outside the Northern Hotel but the substance causing the sticky red fingerprints on it was paint, not human blood. All police leave had been cancelled and, despite working round the clock, the force had, so far, failed to get the vital breakthrough.

At the Monday press conference, Chief Constable Matheson admitted, 'We are really up against it. We just don't appear to be getting the breaks at all.' The killing, which he described as Aberdeen's worst crime, appeared to have been a motiveless act of

27

savagery. June had not been sexually assaulted and robbery was obviously not a motive. He made a special plea to anyone, who may have seen or heard anything suspicious in the area, to come forward at once. Mr Matheson, a Highlander, who had risen through the ranks since joining Aberdeen force as a constable in May 1926, was clearly disappointed that, despite all the publicity, no one had yet come forward to say that they had seen any bloodstained clothing or heard any screams. The trail, he admitted, was getting colder and colder. 'We are just in the dark,' said the Chief.

In a bid to gather every scrap of information, the police asked for the help from the congregations of St Joseph's RC Church, the Salvation Army, the Fountain Mission and Woodside South Church as they would have been going to worship around the time of the murder. Several major questions baffled the murder squad. There was no reason for June to cross Great Northern Road – Kincaid's was on the same side of the street as Printfield Walk – so how did she end up in the lane? And how did she manage to get back over Great Northern Road? Chief Inspector McIntosh was puzzled that only June's footprints were found in the place where she was attacked – a neuk between a hut and a petrol pump.

The search for the murder weapon intensified. Rennie, the tracker dog, and his handler scoured gardens, waste ground and every inch of the murder lane for the weapon, which was described as a 'sharp-edged instrument' and was believed to be a knife or a razor. But they had no luck. Drains were checked and a detective with a metal-detector also failed to find it. But unbeknown to them, the killer had dumped it far from the crime scene.

Descriptions were issued of a number of people who may have been able to help – mostly those of men of various ages. Detectives sought help from pupils at local schools – Woodside, Old Aberdeen, Powis, Tillydrone Primary and Tillydrone Infant. The youngsters were asked the following three questions. Had they see anyone on the Sunday evening with bloodstained hands or clothing?

Had they seen any incident which could be connected with the crime? in the few weeks before June's death, had a stranger offered any of them money in exchange for going off with the person? As we shall see, the significance of this third question was to prove all important.

The parents of the dead child were convinced that someone knew the killer – and was keeping his identity secret. Mr Cruickshank made this dramatic plea through the *Scottish Daily Express*, 'To whoever is sheltering my daughter's killer – for God's sake, please come forward and tell the police all you know before there is another terrible tragedy. Whoever did this must be sick in his mind.' It was signed, 'David K Cruickshank'.

The *Express* left its national rivals far behind with another exclusive story the next day. Aberdeen's taxi 'king', Robert P McIntosh, offered a £1,000 reward for information which would lead to the arrest and conviction of the killer. June's father was a driver with Mr McIntosh's Gallowgate-based company. The story was deliberately omitted from the first edition so that it could not be 'lifted' by rival newspapers. It was 'slipped' into the later Dundee edition and distributed in the Granite City.

In the course of the next few days, the driving rain and sleet turned into a blizzard. Chief Constable Matheson decided to call out the Special Constabulary to calm the fears of mothers with young children. The 'Specials' – their total strength was 135 – were urgently needed to replace tired policemen, some of whom had been drafted in to help the over-stretched CID. Mr Matheson could not rule out the possibility of another attempt on a child's life and, sadly, he was later to be proved right. By the fourth day of the investigation, only two people had responded to a plea for the nineteen possible witnesses to come forward. Mr Matheson's frustration at the lack of public response was summed up in a candid press photograph which showed the perplexed chief scratching his head.

The blinds remained down at the Cruickshanks' flat, as David and Anne got ready to face another harrowing day – June's funeral. Since her death, they had rarely ventured outdoors. Their other children – Brian, Norma (11), Anne Marie (4) and David (2) – were with them. When the youngsters had left the confines of their home they had become the focus of unwanted attention. The Cruickshanks later decided that Anne and their two youngest children should spend a few days with family at Duntocher.

On Friday 13 January – or the 'fifth day of fear' as the *Press and Journal* had called it – newspapers reported the funeral which had taken place the previous day at Trinity Cemetery. The lairs and footpaths of the graveyard were powdered with snow as public and reporters watched the male mourners arrive. The burial was private and only the bereaved were allowed inside the cemetery gates. A press plane circled overhead. Earlier, people had lined the pavement opposite Printfield Walk as the line of four funeral cars passed within a few paces of the spot where the child's body had been found. The cortège turned right on to Great Northern Road, passing the mouth of the lane where June was attacked. Old men doffed their caps and women wept openly.

At Trinity, June's tiny white coffin, topped with wreaths, was borne on the shoulders of two mourners. The tragic but dignified figure of her father walked behind. The small knot of family mourners included June's brother, Brian, his hands clasped in front of him. After a brief ceremony, they returned to Printfield Walk. That dreich evening, the heavens opened and sleet fell on the floral tributes. One came from the dead child's school chums. On the family wreath was a card with a handwritten message, 'With all our love. Mum and Daddy, Brian, Norma, Anne and David.'

On the Saturday following the murder, the man leading the hunt made a loudspeaker appeal to the 20,000 spectators during the interval at the Scottish League Division One match between the Dons and Celtic at Pittodrie. No new witnesses came forward but Chief Inspector McIntosh's plea touched the hearts of a group

30

of Celtic supporters who went and laid a wreath on June's grave before heading back to Glasgow.

The police and the public were mystified by the reluctance of witnesses to come forward. One week after the murder, thirty-five witnesses had still not answered the desperate pleas for help. Interestingly, a bloodstained man had been spotted on a town-bound bus on the evening of the murder. The passenger, who had blood on his forehead and face, was on a No. 18 bus travelling from the direction of Smithfield. He got off in Castle Street and walked towards Marischal Street but changed his mind and turned to go in the direction of the Salvation Army Citadel. One theory was that the man could be a seaman heading for the harbour area but a check of boats failed to turn up anything. The city was swept with rumours of girls being attacked. An anonymous postcard was delivered to the *Press and Journal*. It read: 'A car was used. Police should concitrate [sic] on this, also man had local knowledge.' It was treated with caution by investigators.

Detectives investigated a complaint that a four-year-old girl, coincidentally also named June, had been enticed away from near her home in Logie Avenue, which is less than two miles from Printfield. The girl, like June Cruickshank before her, had been sent on an errand by her mother to a nearby shop. She was found safe and well an hour later, after her alleged young abductor had fled. It later transpired that there was no connection between this incident and the murder but parents, who were already anxious, became even more frightened and the streets of the nearby housing estates of Middlefield and Northfield were empty of children before dark. Middlefield Primary School was said to have closed its doors and ordered its pupils home after two girls had been attacked. It was, however, a half-truth. The school had shut down but it was actually because burst water pipes had flooded classrooms.

When rumour-mongers spread 'wild and hurtful' lies about the murder, the Rev. J R MacCulloch, the Cruickshank family's minister, lashed out at them from the pulpit of Bon-Accord Church.

But, in the midst of suspicion, fear and innuendo, plain-clothes detectives and bobbies in diced caps got on with their work, which was described by their chief constable as 'dead slogging and hard plodding'. I stood at the corner of Great Northern Road and Printfield Walk and watched as a girl of June's age, a policeman's daughter, re-enacted the dead girl's last moments as she walked from the Cruickshanks' home to the corner shop and then to the place where the body was found. It proved that June had taken longer to cover the distance than had at first been thought. Chief Inspector McIntosh, who was present, said that the minutes of June's life after she left home probably approached fifteen rather than ten.

There was a flurry of excitement when two Aberdeen detectives flew to London to question a night porter, a Scot, who, at one time, had lived in Aberdeen. But, after being held overnight at Paddington police station, he was cleared. Meanwhile, in a bid to get the reluctant witnesses to come forward, Chief Constable Matheson travelled to the BBC studios in Glasgow to record a television interview, the first of its kind ever given by a Scottish Chief Constable. Mr Matheson frankly admitted to reporter Norman Thomson that his force was making little headway in the investigation. He pleaded with the missing witnesses, both men and women, to make themselves known and he calmed any fears they might have about talking to the police. If a reluctant witness wrote to him personally with their name and address, he would send an officer to take their statement. But Mr Matheson's dramatic plea was met with a lukewarm response, with only a handful of people coming forward, none of whom were able to cast new light on the investigation. The reluctance of potentially vital witnesses to help prompted Highland novelist Jane Duncan, whose father had been a policeman, to write an impassioned letter to the *Press and Journal*. She urged people to come forward to help solve 'the most depraved' of all crimes – child murder – otherwise everyone was an accessory to murder.

While in Glasgow, Mr Matheson had talks with his opposite number in Paisley. They believed there might be a link between the Aberdeen murder and the slaying of six-year-old David Hutton in a Paisley park in August 1960. Even in their hour of renewed grief, the dead boy's parents had sent a letter of sympathy to the Cruickshanks. The upshot was that Detective Inspector Tom Goodall, one of Glasgow's top detectives, who had helped put a noose around the neck of Peter Manuel, a mass murderer, and Detective Inspector Fred Pender, of Paisley CID, came to Aberdeen and inspected the murder scene. The police hinted at similarities between the two crimes but said no more. The detectives from the West of Scotland stayed one night in the city and didn't return.

During the intensive murder hunt, police had interviewed between 10,000 and 15,000 people and checked on the movements of many thousands more. Boxes, bursting with paperwork, were stacked from floor to ceiling along two walls in a CID office at police headquarters. It seemed as if their teamwork had been all for nothing. Yet, unbeknown to the public, the murder squad team were clinging to a vital clue that would eventually nail the killer. The clue had turned up when June's distraught mother hurried to her dying daughter's side. A female bystander had spotted a gleam of silver lying beside the body. It was a one-shilling piece. During the few moments she had been at the murder scene, the woman had come to understand that the girl had been sent on an errand. So she handed the shilling to Mrs Cruickshank, assuming it was change that June had dropped. But this was not the case – the coin had been given to June by her killer. And, before he was caught, the killer would strike again and the trail that had begun in Woodside in January 1961 would eventually lead police across the city to Heading Hill.

3

LAIR

1963

The streets of Aberdeen resembled the joke postcard showing a deserted Union Street on a flag day. The trades-holiday fortnight was in full swing as Aberdonians went in search of the sun, with Spain the most popular destination. But, for young stay-at-home George Forbes, it offered the opportunity of exploring favourite harbour haunts near his home. Seven-year-old George loved pigeons and would go to derelict property and sheds at the docks to feed the birds.

At 7 p.m. on Sunday 7 July 1963, the pale, dark-haired boy left home at 46 Justice Street with a cheerful, 'Cheerio, I won't be long' in sign language to his deaf mother, Mrs Mary Forbes (42), and his unemployed father, John (also in his forties), who could neither speak nor hear. George, the youngest in a family of four, ran downstairs to play and that was the last time his parents saw him. He was wearing a blue-flecked V-neck pullover, grey shirt, light khaki shorts and black gym shoes.

Police concentrated the hunt for him over a radius of one mile from his tenement home on the corner of Justice Street and Commerce Street. Because many premises in the dockland area were closed for the holiday, the owners were asked to come and unlock their properties to allow police to carry out checks. This was to make sure that the boy had not fallen and injured himself while climbing. Sniffer dogs, Rennie and Colonel, and their handlers checked the area at the beach and the Broad Hill. The missing boy's father joined the search and his three other children,

34

Billy (14), Helen (12) and Kenneth (10), along with some friends, did their bit.

Police had two reported sightings of George. A boy answering his description had been spotted in Park Street, near Frederick Street, less than an hour after he had left home. He was with two boys of his own age who were sucking lollipops or sweets. The second sighting was more worrying. A woman, who knew George, had reported seeing him 'capering about' on rocks at the North Pier at the harbour entrance. The sighting was corroborated by another witness and police feared he may have met with an accident and drowned. In the light of no other information, the statements were written up and destined for the files. But cruelty was in the air the evening George vanished and none of us, who gathered on the pavement outside his home for an impromptu press briefing by detectives, realised at the time that the boy was buried in a rough grave only about 100 yards away.

Two days after he had apparently vanished into thin air, the main story being filed by reporters in Aberdeen concerned the Roman Catholic Bishop of Aberdeen's refusal to sack his house-keeper, Mrs Christine MacKenzie. A divorcée who had been married to a Church of Scotland minister, Mrs MacKenzie (42) had been made the target of hate mail, anonymous phone calls and malicious gossip by a few people in the diocese. When the rumours concerning Mrs MacKenzie found their way to the Vatican, the bishop in question, the Right Rev. Dr Francis Walsh (61), was ordered to dismiss her. He considered the edict to be 'unjust and cruel' and refused to comply with it. Instead, he staunchly defended his housekeeper against the unfounded accusations. When the Vatican refused to relent and insisted she must go, Bishop Walsh, an honourable man, resigned and moved to Ireland where he stayed until his death.

Four months later, on Saturday 16 November, as workers hurried home for lunch, police, 'acting on certain information', arrived at a ramshackle greenhouse in an allotment behind

Castlehill. Detectives picked their way through the rows of cabbages, down the steep embankment and past a crude hand-painted 'Veges for sale' sign went into the greenhouse through a lean-to entrance. The steep slope was a fragment of Heading Hill, which was linked to Castlehill by an iron bridge. It spanned busy Commerce Street, which was the valley 'betwixt the hillis' where the public hangman, John Justice, had executed twenty-three witches and one warlock during the year 1596–7 for a fee of 6s 8d per victim.

As plain-clothes men, wearing gumboots and blue and green dungarees and carrying spades, began digging up the earthen floor of the greenhouse, a handful of passers-by gathered at the seven-foot-high barbed-wire fence surrounding the allotment. The onlookers were told that the search was for stolen property. The city's new Chief Constable, William Smith, and Detective Chief Inspector Harry Halcrow were also at the scene. Mr Smith had succeeded Alexander Matheson, who had died on 14 March 1963. His death, at the early age of fifty-eight, meant that, sadly, Mr Matheson would not see the killer of June Cruickshank brought to justice. Soon afterwards, the procurator fiscal, Mr Andrew S McNicol, the Crown's appointed prosecutor, arrived.

During the digging, a fire engine drew up. The firemen were told to stand by in case police were affected by sewage gas during their excavations. In the fading afternoon light, the flashbulbs of police photographers lit up the gloomy greenhouse interior. Then a hearse pulled into a nearby cul-de-sac. It was sent away and, in its place, a blue van arrived. After about four hours, I watched, with Bill Beattie, my *Scottish Daily Express* colleague, as detectives, dirt-streaked and perspiring, carried a bundle, covered with a black plastic tarpaulin, to the waiting van. Its next stop was the police mortuary at Lodge Walk. The fiscal, who had spent over two hours in the greenhouse with police surgeons Douglas McBain and William Hendry, told us, 'All I can say at the moment is that, acting on certain information, police officers went to this particular site. They have uncovered remains which, at first hand, appear to be the body of a young boy. I can say no more until a post-mortem has been carried out.' That post-mortem was held the following day and the boy's parents called at police headquarters to identify the clothes that George had been wearing when he vanished. There was an added ordeal for Mr and Mrs Forbes which they would have to endure until they moved to another address. The kitchen window of their third-floor flat overlooked the killer's lair – the greenhouse where their son's body had been buried. After confirming that the body found in the shallow grave was George's, Mr McNicol said a man would appear in court on the Monday in connection with the death. On that bright Sunday afternoon, I flew over the murder scene in a chartered light aircraft with *Express* photographer Ron Taylor.

On Monday 18 November, the man police arrested was named as James John Oliphant (39), an Aberdeen labourer. He was awaiting trial when his fortieth birthday came round. His brief appearance before Sheriff Aikman Smith warranted large black type in newspaper headlines. He was formally charged with the double murder of George Forbes and June Cruickshank. He was also charged with three offences of indecency and one of assault, all of which involved young children. He was remanded for further inquiries. This dramatic news brought unimaginable grief for the Cruickshanks. They had moved to a new home in Kincorth, where June's dad, David, had taken to his bed, suffering from stress.

Oliphant had been escorted before the sheriff by Detective Chief Inspector Halcrow, Detective Inspector Tom Cobb and Detective Sergeant Bill Adams, a future Deputy Chief Constable of Grampian Police (1983–87). Mr Halcrow and Detective Inspector Hamish Johnston, who had been deeply involved in the Woodside murder hunt, later went to Mrs Cruickshank's work to inform her of Oliphant's arrest. They drove the distraught mother home to be with her family. When he appeared in the dock at a Sheriff Court Pleading Diet on Monday 3 February 1964, Oliphant, balding, powerfully built and known to his workmates as 'Big Jim', sat with downcast eyes, his huge hands clasped in front of him. When asked by Sheriff Archibald Hamilton how he was to plead to the indictment of six charges, including the culpable homicides of June and George, the ruddy-faced Highlander replied, 'Guilty, sir.' Oliphant betrayed no emotion during the 30-minute hearing as Mr McNicol, the fiscal, told the court the accused had killed June and George because they screamed.

The fiscal began his story on 8 January 1961 when June's mother, preparing a meal, discovered she needed some custard powder. She gave June sixpence and sent her to Kincaid's corner shop. Later, June was found in the street, apparently unconscious and badly hurt, and the woman, who had found her, thought she had been struck by a vehicle. Seeing the small crowd gather in the street, Mrs Cruickshank, who was worried about the length of time her daughter had been gone, went to investigate. The fiscal went on, 'A woman among the bystanders saw a shilling lying beside the body and handed it to Mrs Cruickshank, assuming the girl had dropped it. Mrs Cruickshank was in a very distressed state and, without thinking about it, put the shilling in her pocket.'

Mr McNicol described the huge police manhunt for the killer and how, despite this, they had failed to net their man. The strangest thing, he told the court, was that the police could not trace anybody who had seen June cross Great Northern Road after the terrible wound had been inflicted. 'The police kept the file open and kept a careful watch for any further information,' he told in the hushed courtroom. 'When they went back to Mrs Cruickshank, she remembered the shilling.' She was convinced she had only given June sixpence – and the police, it will be remembered, found the halfpenny change under her body. The existence of this shilling was known to only a handful of people. The find was not noted or made public at the time. 'It might, of course, have been just a casual shilling, dropped by a passer-by,' said the fiscal. The police kept the information to themselves, realising that it might prove to be a vital clue.

Mr McNicol then switched the scene to the evening of Armistice Day 1963 – four months after George Forbes vanished – when the father of a seven-year-old boy noticed that his son had a red welt around his neck. The boy said that he and his pal had been in a shed on an allotment in Castlehill and that Oliphant, whom they knew as Jimmy, had put a rope round his neck, looped the other end over a hook and pulled. The man took his son to the police. They questioned the boy's chum and he confirmed that the incident had, indeed, taken place. He said he had been alarmed by what had happened and that he had feared Oliphant was going to tie the other end of the rope round his neck. He had escaped from the shed into the adjoining greenhouse and, from there, he had escaped through a hole.

In the course of routine inquiries, as they always do in cases that potentially involve indecency, the police asked if the boys knew of any other children who had been to the allotment. One child made a remark about George Forbes but later denied any knowledge of the missing boy being present. Police interviewed Oliphant about the assault on the boy with the neck wound and, when he was asked if he knew anything about George Forbes, Oliphant replied, 'Will it make it any easier on me if I tell you? I'll take you to where that loon Forbes is. He's down at my greenhouse. He started screaming and I cut his throat with a knife.' A post-mortem showed that his throat had been cut in almost exactly the same manner as that of June Cruickshank.

Detectives then quizzed Oliphant about June and – said Mr McNicol – he replied, 'Aye, it was me. I gave her a shilling. I took her round the back of the petrol place. Later she started screaming. I ken I'll get hung for this. I'm finished.' Then, said the fiscal, Oliphant began to cry.

At the time of June's death, Oliphant had been the gaffer of a small squad of corporation men who were working near the place where the girl's body was found. The reason he was not suspected was that he lived in Market Street, which is a fair distance from the murder scene. During this period, his workmates told police that Oliphant's behaviour had been perfectly normal. The unmasking of Oliphant as a double killer, the court heard, was due solely to the very careful investigations by Aberdeen City Police in following up the most slender of clues. 'None of the other children was hurt in any way,' said Mr McNicol. 'In view of Oliphant's reply, one could only be thankful that none of them had screamed.' After consulting psychiatric reports, Sheriff Hamilton sent Oliphant to the High Court – which was due to meet in Aberdeen eight days later – for sentence.

Oliphant maintained his sphinx-like expression when he returned to the same courtroom on 11 February. Mr James Law, advocate-depute, told the judge, Lord Strachan, that the charges relating to June and George were originally ones of murder but they had been reduced to culpable homicide because of Oliphant's diminished responsibility. Oliphant also admitted lewd practices towards other children and, during the hearing, it was said that he always gave a shilling to the youngsters to buy sweets before committing offences against them. Oliphant had been trapped by the shilling he gave one of his victims – June Cruickshank. Medical witnesses warned that, if he was ever set free, there was a chance he might kill again.

Oliphant shut his eyes for several minutes as the medical reports were read out. Psychiatrist, Dr James Henderson, said that a sexual relationship between Oliphant and his stepfather, which had been forced on him as a boy, had had a lasting effect on him. When he was a child in Caithness, he claimed his stepfather gagged and bound him and beat him with a stick so that the stepfather could satisfy his sexual perversions. This resulted in him trying to force others to suffer as he himself had suffered as a child. He had told Dr Henderson, 'There is a queer feeling that happens to me at times. It has bothered me since I was young – a cold, shivery feeling, especially when I see blood.' At no time did Oliphant show any remorse for his actions and nor did he express any concern for the relatives of the children involved.

He had had a three-year romance with a waitress he had met in a city dance hall in the early 1950s but she had died of heart trouble. He was heartbroken. Dr Henderson quoted Oliphant as saying, 'I never had any friends. The only time I had any friends was in a pub when I had money. I was often out at nights, wandering on my own. Most evenings I went to the plot, then went upstairs to my room and read the papers.' Dr Andrew Wyllie, physician superintendent of Cornhill Hospital, said Oliphant, who was of low intelligence, had been certified as mentally defective in 1942. He called the killings 'infanto-sexual sadism' – a form of sexual perversion in which sexual gratification was gained by inflicting cruelty upon others.

Oliphant, who was born near Wick, didn't know his father. He was the eldest of a family of eight children and, after being sexually abused by his stepfather, he had run away from home and school and had ended up in an approved school in Aberdeen. He returned to Caithness to work on a farm, where he one of his duties was slaughtering pigs by cutting their throats. He also worked as a horseman on the farm and he always carried a sharp knife. 'If a horse fell, he might use it to cut the animal free from its harness,' said Dr Wyllie. Three years before he was arrested, Oliphant had been working with Aberdeen Corporation Sewage Department. He was not interviewed by police and he was afraid to come forward. If he had been quizzed, he might have broken down and confessed. It is my belief that, had Oliphant not been discounted because of his Market Street address, perhaps George Forbes would not have become a victim.

James Law, advocate-depute, then asked the doctor, 'If he were to be set at large, might he, as a result of his mental disorder, commit offences again?' and Dr Wyllie replied, 'I am of the opinion that he would be liable to commit such offences again.' Lord Strachan, giving his verdict, decided that Oliphant would be sent to Carstairs State Mental Hospital 'without limit of time'. A Crown spokesman in Edinburgh told *Scottish Daily Express* reporter Bill Beattie that the term 'without limit of time' meant, in effect, a life sentence to a mental hospital. The only person who could free Oliphant was the Scottish Secretary and that could only happen if he felt there were good grounds for his release in years to come. But he added, 'This is hardly likely under the circumstances.' With hindsight, was Oliphant the blood-stained man who got off the No. 18 bus in Castle Street on the night of June Cruickshank's murder? He was last seen walking towards the Citadel. Was he heading for his plot to wash away the evidence of his crime before returning to his digs? Oliphant lived in the loft of a comfortable, top-floor flat that was occupied by a couple and their schoolboy son. The flat was above a bank at the bottom of Market Street. Oliphant slept in an iron cot in the cluttered loft which was reached by a ladder. After the address was published, the landlady turned down a request by a well-dressed businessman who wanted to sleep in the cot.

They were stacking away the June Cruickshank files in the cellars of the police headquarters when Adam Borthwick, chief reporter of the *Scottish Daily Express* in north-east Scotland, spoke to Detective Chief Inspector Halcrow about the secret one shilling clue inherited from ex-CID boss Donald McIntosh. The coin, sealed and labelled in an envelope, was destined for the force's 'black museum'. Why was there no mention of the vital clue in the hue and cry following June's violent death? 'It is an old-fashioned maxim to keep something to oneself,' said Mr Halcrow. 'No card-player ever reveals his hand, even in a jam.' If someone was eventually caught, the police had to be convinced that he was responsible – and the shilling would reveal a vital fact. That was the reasoning behind many investigations. 'Exact amounts of money are never disclosed,' added Mr Halcrow. So the clue became all important when Big Jim Oliphant confessed he had given June a shilling.

Mr Halcrow paid tribute to the teamwork of the force at the time of the two murders. He told me that it was a combined operation by all ranks. He revealed that, when Oliphant was arrested for assaulting the boy in his greenhouse, it was a young uniformed constable who had reminded the CID of the boy, George Forbes, who had disappeared and was presumed to have fallen off the rocks at the North Pier. The young officer remembered that the boy's body had never been found. Mr Halcrow had the officer transferred to the CID as a reward for his part in helping to bring the double killer to justice.

One evening shortly after Oliphant was convicted, George's parents and June's parents met each other for the first time. Mr and Mrs Cruickshank went to the Forbes' home in Justice Street. It was a poignant occasion, during which they shared their mutual grief over a pot of tea.

Oliphant died in Carstairs in 1988. His death was confirmed by the Scottish Office on 1 March. His allotment disappeared after Commerce Street was widened and road improvements also resulted in the Forbes' house being demolished. The family was subsequently rehoused.

And the sinister cul-de-sac, where June Cruickshank met her tragic end, and Kincaid's shop, where she bought custard powder, are no more.

HANGMAN'S BRAE

The day after the body of George Forbes was exhumed from Oliphant's allotment, the *Scottish Daily Express* informed its readers that the greenhouse was only a few steps from the defunct Hangman's Brae, which had been absorbed by Castle Terrace in the nineteenth century. The burgh hangman had lived in the vicinity. He had occupied a house, known as 'Hangman's Hoose' in Canal Terrace, on the east bank of the old canal, which was crossed by a bridge dubbed 'Hangman's Brig'. Hangman's Brae, a steep, narrow, walled path, paved with blue causey stones, led to the Castlegate gallows. Aberdeen's most famous hangman, Johnny Milne, a drystone dyker, took the job in 1806 rather than face transportation for life for stealing beehives at Tillyskukie farm on Donside. He was paid £7 10s for a half-year's salary. The perks of his job included a free house, grazing for his pony around St Clement's Kirkyard and, on market day, a fish out of every creel, a peat from every cart load and a ladle of meal from every sack.

4

THE ABERDEEN SACK MURDER

1934

Under a brooding sky in April 1934, housewife Jeannie Donald accompanied her nimble-footed schoolgirl daughter, also called Jeannie, on whom she doted, from their home to an evening dress rehearsal at the Beach Pavilion. This was a cosy, intimate concert hall, situated across from the Links and overlooking the cold, grey North Sea. Wee Jeannie, a nine-year-old pupil of King Street Public School, would rehearse five dance numbers, which meant she would wear the five different frocks that her mother had spent part of that afternoon ironing.

The dress rehearsal began at 6.30 p.m. and Jeannie dutifully performed her numbers, which included Highland dancing, toe-dancing, ballet and two other pieces. One was entitled 'Dancing Night' and the other was called 'Sleepy Town' – a somewhat ironic title, given the way events were to unfold. It was 11 p.m. when the final curtain fell. Mrs Donald's husband, Alexander, a hairdresser, had arranged to meet his wife and daughter after work but, as it turned out, he had only managed to catch the last two hours of the show. It was raining heavily that night and a bitterly cold wind blew down rain-slicked streets. Mr Donald greeted his wife and daughter with the news that a crowd had gathered outside their home in Urquhart Road, a chasm of grey granite tenements that runs from the beach links, in the east, to busy King Street, in the west. He hadn't gone into the house – the Donalds were already aware why the crowd was there. Helen Priestly, the eight-year-old only child of the couple who lived in the flat directly above them, had been reported missing earlier that day. The fair-haired girl was last seen approaching the street door of No. 61 at 1.30 p.m.

Friday 20 April 1934, had been a busy day for the Donalds. Mrs Donald (38) rose at 6.45 a.m., washed and got dressed. She then went to the nearby Co-op baker for morning rowies. She started to make breakfast, polish shoes and clean the fireside grate. Her husband (also 38) left to go to McKillip's shop in King Street and Jeannie got ready to go to school, a few minutes' walk to the west of their home. At lunch-time, Mr Donald and little Jeannie hurried home to be fed. After running an errand to the Co-op, Jeannie met her father on his way back to work. Shortly afterwards, Jeannie, clutching her gym shoes, left for school with her chum, Netta Esson, both sucking sugared almonds given to them by Jeannie's mother.

At tea-time, Mr Donald returned home to eat before hurrying back to cut hair in the gents' salon. When his wife told him that Helen had gone missing after being sent on an errand, he replied, somewhat indifferently, 'She's lost her money and been feart to come hame.' There was no love lost between Mrs Donald and Mrs Priestly. They had not been on friendly terms for a number of years. Two or three months before she vanished, Helen had told her mother how Mrs Donald had come out of her door and followed her with her eyes as she had climbed the stairs. Mrs Priestly had told her to ignore her. Helen had a disrespectful nickname for Mrs Donald – 'Coconut' – but why she called her this is uncertain. Mr Priestly passed it off as 'old-fashionedness' and said their neighbour was just a 'nosey parker'.

By the time the Donald family had arrived home from the Pavilion, the crowd had grown. The Donalds did not recognise any of the faces. Mrs Donald's thin-lipped mouth tightened as they pushed their way past the jostling crowd and to the front door of No. 61, which stands on the north side of the street. The front door opened from the pavement on to a common lobby, on either side of which were two ground-floor flats. For the past seven years, the Donalds had lived in the flat on the right-hand side of the lobby. Their comfortable parlour was at the front of the house. It was a high, gas-lit room, with dark leather chairs, a high mirrored wardrobe, a potted aspidistra, a table draped with a chenille-fringed cloth and walls hung with paintings of Highland scenes. There was also a gas fire and a bed. When they had visitors in the summer, they would be accommodated in this room. But the family ate and slept in the kitchen, which overlooked the communal drying green at the back. The kitchen was furnished with a table, chairs, a mirrored dresser and, within a curtained recess, there was a bed where all three of them slept. There was a gramophone at the back of the kitchen door. There was also a sink below the window and, under the sink, a double-doored cupboard. Behind the door on the left was a coal-scuttle, while the larger press on the right held soap powder, bleach, brushes and a wooden cinder-box.

After drinking tea, the Donalds went to bed. Mr Donald slept next to the wall, his wife slept on the outside and wee Jeannie lay snugly between them. At midnight, a policeman knocked on their door and asked for the keys to their coal cellar in the back yard and to the cubby-hole in a recess under the stairs. Mr Donald pulled on his trousers, handed over the keys and came back to bed a few minutes later. The policeman who had called for the keys was Detective Constable Alexander Matheson. He was the Chief Constable of Aberdeen at the time of the June Cruickshank murder hunt in 1961. Sleep was barely possible for the couple although Jeannie slept undisturbed. In the course of that dreadful, rain-lashed night, footsteps drummed on the stairs as people came and went in search of Helen Priestly.

Helen, a shy, well-behaved girl, who had been warned not to talk to strangers, had been sent by her mother to buy a 4d plain half loaf at the Co-op during her school lunch-break. A fellow pupil saw Helen a few steps from No. 61 but did not see if she entered. Helen's mum, Mrs Agnes Priestly (33) became worried when her only child did not return and she went searching for her. She knew that Helen was always anxious to return to school after lunch. Mrs Priestly called at the Co-op where she was told her daughter had bought the bread. She had left with the loaf wrapped in paper and her mum's 'Co-opie' cheque – all Co-op stores issued these with each purchase and the money spent was recorded to be paid out in an annual 'divvy' or dividend. An anxious Mrs Priestly hurried to King Street School, where the pupils were about to file inside for the afternoon session. In the playground, she spoke to wee Jeannie Donald who went off to look for Helen but she couldn't find her. Mrs Priestly spread word of her daughter's disappearance and a family friend, Helen Robertson, who was Helen's godmother, went to the police. Mrs Priestly broke the news to her husband, John (47), a painter and decorator, who was on a job at the Saltoun Arms – the public house, where Harrow had attacked two of his fellow butchers in 1901.

In the ensuing hue and cry, a fellow pupil and playmate of the missing girl reported seeing Helen being abducted. The little boy told Mr Priestly that his daughter had been dragged on to a tram car by a man. He later told detectives that the stranger was middle-aged, 5 feet 10 inches tall and dressed in a dark coat with a tear in the back. Helen was carrying a loaf and wearing her blue tammy. No time was wasted in circulating these descriptions. A variety programme from the Aberdeen BBC radio studio was interrupted. Messages were flashed up on cinema screens. The hunt spread to Bridge of Don and Bridge of Dee. Asylums were checked to see if any of their patients were missing.

As Mr Priestly and friends and neighbours joined police in the search for Helen and her abductor, a heavy downpour lashed the city. A man, whose two-year-old daughter had been abducted the previous October but who was later found safe at Cairncry quarry, also offered to help. William Duncan (39), a friend of Mr Priestly, drove him round the city in his car and the pair asked people on the streets if they had seen Helen in the company of the stranger that the little boy had described. Unfortunately, nobody had seen them. The general search was called off at around 1 a.m. on 21 April and would resume at 5 a.m.

Next morning, the police pressed the boy for more details of Helen's abductor and he admitted that his story had been a complete fabrication, based on what he had been told by other boys. Although he had been in Urquhart Road on his way to school the previous lunch-time, he had not seen Helen. Precious time had been wasted in pursuing Helen and her bogus abductor and, by the time the boy had confessed, the child's body had been found on the floor of the lobby of No 61. The number 21657, from the 'Co-opie' carbon voucher, was imprinted on the palm of her right hand.

It was a fine, clear morning when William Duncan came back in his car to collect Mr Priestly and resume the search. Fellow searcher, Alexander Porter (48), who lived on the opposite side of the street, walked into No. 61 but rushed out again shouting, 'The body's in the bag at the back of the lobby.' The sack, a jute bag, lay close to the back door. It was in a recess between the door of the ground-floor toilet and the cubby- hole under the stairs. The child's feet were protruding from the untied mouth of the sack, which bore the letters 'BOSS' painted in red. Eight families lived in the four-floored tenement and, within minutes, the place was in uproar, with screaming and thumping on doors. Duncan hammered on the doors of the ground-floor tenants, the Topps and the Donalds. Shopkeeper William Topp (29) had set the alarm for 4 a.m. and had left half an hour later. His wife, Mary (28), who was expecting, fell into a deep sleep after a wakeful night. But she was wakened by the terrible screams of Mrs Priestly, 'Oh, John, ma bairn, ma bairn!' During the commotion, Mrs Topp became racked with sickness and pain and then she fainted. The shock would later cause her to suffer a miscarriage.

However, at this point, there was no sign of the Donalds. They were awake in bed when Mrs Priestly's screams brought a response from Mrs Donald to her husband. 'Oh, rise and see what's ado, Alex,' she said. He replied, 'Na na, na na, ye ken she's hysterical and she will be wantin' out to look for her kiddie and they will be keeping her back.' Mrs Donald would later claim that she heard an upstairs neighbour, old Mrs Joss, cry, 'She's been used, she's been used!' But nobody else could remember hearing those words or uttering them. Once it was quiet in the lobby, Mr Donald pulled on his coat and went to collect the milk. He asked Constable John Cassie, the first policeman on the scene, 'Is there any word?'. Cassie told him, 'She's been found in a sack in the lobby.' Mr Donald replied, 'Oh!' and went back inside. The sack and the girl's clothing were dry, yet there was a pool of rainwater outside the back door and the back green was soft, with no footprints. There had been a lot of to-ing and fro-ing during the night so there was little or no chance of a stranger slipping in through the street door with the sack. Constable Cassie spotted that the mouth of the sack was not wrinkled, so it had not been carried over the shoulder for any distance. A kink at the level of the child's abdomen suggested that it had been carried over the arm. (Cassie's farm background helped him in deducing such things.) The child's new tammy and knickers were missing. She wore a gilt bracelet on her right forearm. Police would later photograph her in situ.

The murder must have been committed in the tenement and, because the child appeared to have been strangled and raped, the menfolk who lived in the building were the chief suspects. But they all had cast-iron alibis, having been at work at the time. At the subsequent trial, the cause of death was established as asphyxiation through vomiting. The sexual-assault theory proved incorrect. The suspicion was that the injury to her private parts had been inflicted to simulate rape. News of the grim discovery of the 'Aberdeen Sack Murder' in the lobby and rumours that Helen had been 'outraged and suffocated' caused a sensation. Huge crowds from all parts of the city and even beyond descended on Urquhart Road. In their hunt for clues, the police combed 'the

Jungle', a complex of allotments with dog kennels, huts, poultry runs and garages. After they had checked each rickety building, they chalked a white cross on its door.

Detective Constable John Westland, who later became head of the CID in Aberdeen, interviewed the Donalds in their home on 25 April. Mrs Donald expressed her willingness to help and answered the questions freely, although the fingers of her large hands drummed incessantly on the table. She gave a detailed account of events on the day of Helen's murder, from the time she awoke to the grim discovery of the body. She said she had left the house at 1.10 or 1.15 in the afternoon and walked to The Green, the weekly open-air market, that is still held in the cobbled square behind Union Street. She bought a dozen eggs from Davidson, of Alford, for either 10d or 11d. She next called at Rezin's stall and paid sixpence for six oranges. She made her way to Correction Wynd, named after the house of correction that once stood here, to St Nicholas Street and 'Raggie' Morrison's – Morrison's Economic Stores . She priced some material for a frock for her daughter, then walked home where she saw several people, including a tearful Mrs Priestly, standing at the grocer's opposite No. 61.

Mrs Donald was inside the front door of the tenement when Mrs Topp, who had been washing her windows at the back, pushed open the back door. 'I am back early,' said Mrs Donald. They did not mention the missing girl. At the time they took Mrs Donald's statement, the police had not made up their minds to arrest the couple. But they were given permission to search the house and reddish stains were found at the bottom of a cupboard.

Police surgeon Dr Robert Richards, Lecturer in Forensic Medicine at Aberdeen University, who had helped carry out the post-mortem, believed that the stains were blood. The police arrested the couple and charged them with murder. Mrs Donald replied, 'I did not do that.' Her husband said he was not guilty. The Donalds were escorted through a hostile crowd to a waiting 'Black Maria'. Press cameras flashed from an upstairs window across the street. Castle Street was choked with crowds waiting to see the police van arrive at Lodge Walk. Excited shouts and loud jeering erupted from the throng.

Scrapings of the stains found in the cupboard were chemically examined by Dr Richards and they were found not to be blood. There was, however, no question of releasing the Donalds. When they briefly appeared before a sheriff on a murder charge, Mrs Donald was drawn and haggard. Her slightly built husband was kept in custody for six weeks before police were convinced of his innocence. Mrs Donald's trip to The Green had taken place a week earlier. The prices she said she had paid were not in force on 20 April but they did tally with those on offer the previous week. Mrs Priestly and the other women had been in the street across from No. 61 but Mrs Donald could have known this because she had spied on them from her front window. She could have lurked inside the street door, to fool Mrs Topp into believing she had just returned from shopping. Be that as it may, the Crown would have to rely on forensic evidence to win its case. Professor (later Sir) Sydney Smith, of the Chair of Forensic Medicine at Edinburgh University, was a star witness for the prosecution. In his time, he was regarded as a world authority in his field. In Aberdeen, he linked up with Professor Theodore Shennan, of the Chair of Pathology at Aberdeen University, and his colleague, Dr Richards, and carried out tests on certain articles found at the scene of the murder. Professor John Glaister, of the Chair of Forensic Medicine at Glasgow University, was another medical witness. Their evidence proved vital during the six-day High Court murder trial which began on Monday 16 July. However, because of the wave of ill-feeling towards the accused in the Granite City, the venue was switched to Edinburgh in the interests of justice.

The sack containing the body had a hole in the top left-hand corner. Empty sacks found in the cubby-hole below the stairs had holes in the same place which suggested that the BOSS sack had hung on the same peg. Fibres from the death sack matched fluff and cinders found in the Donalds' house and there was human hair which might have been Mrs Donald's. The wooden cinder-box under the sink had disappeared but cinders were found in the dead child's mouth and hair. It was here the body had lain hidden. A rectangular-shaped mark formed by ashes and dust on the linoleum on the floor of the cupboard under the sink indicated where the cinder box had stood. It was never recovered.

Mrs Donald showed little emotion while listening to the evidence. The women jurors recoiled in horror when the victim's post-mortem organs and body tissue, preserved in glass bottles, was shown to a witness – but the accused was undisturbed by the macabre exhibits. However, her mask slipped when her daughter, Jeannie, unwittingly gave evidence which linked her mother to the sordid crime. Jeannie said that she did not recognise the kind of bread – a plain half loaf – Helen had bought at the Co-op. However, part of a plain loaf had been found in the Donald's home – and Jeannie said her mother always bought a 'French' loaf. Jeannie also described the cinder-box under the sink but could not remember when she last saw it. The scientists were able to confirm that the stains found on a copy of the *Aberdeen Evening Express* of 19 April were blood. And there were also traces of blood on a packet of soap flakes, a scrubbing brush, a washing cloth and a portion of linoleum from under the sink. These were all Helen's blood type – group O. But this disclosure carried limited weight as between 40 and 50 per cent of people are in that group.

Professor Thomas Mackie, a top bacteriologist at Edinburgh University, discovered a rare type of intestinal germ on what remained of Helen's torn white cotton underclothes and also on the washing cloth found in the accused's kitchen. His considered opinion was that the items had been contaminated from the same source. This disclosure was of great significance to the outcome of the trial. In his address to the jury, the Lord Justice Clerk, the Right Hon. Lord Aitchison, said that they might think it a very remarkable coincidence but it was 'a very small fact if you measure it with a foot-rule, because the thing is microscopic, but it may be a tremendously significant fact in this case'.

Mrs Donald did not give evidence. After seventeen minutes the jury returned their verdict – 'Guilty of murder by a majority'. Mrs Donald broke down in the dock. Smelling-salts and a glass of water barely revived her and she was carried moaning from the court. She was sentenced to hang at Craiginches Prison on 13 August but an appeal saw her conviction reduced to penal servitude for life. (Lord Provost Henry Alexander personally delivered the news.) Two days after she was due to hang, two female officers escorted Mrs Donald on foot to the Joint Station where they caught a train for Glasgow. No one recognised her. Her final destination was Duke Street Prison.

Why did Mrs Donald kill Helen? In his memoirs, Sir Sydney Smith assumed that, when Helen had re-entered the lobby, she made some objectionable remark to the woman. This had angered Mrs Donald and she had seized the girl by the throat and had shaken her, with tragic results. The post-mortem had revealed that Helen had had a physical defect – an enlarged thymus – which, in the circumstances of Mrs Donald grasping her round the neck, would have caused the child to lose consciousness. Mrs Donald, believing she had killed the girl, had then panicked. She had carried the inert body into her house where she faked rape with an instrument. But Helen, who was not dead, screamed in pain. Death was due to asphyxiation, which had apparently been caused by compression of the neck. Another theory was that she had choked on vomit or food. It had been her cry that a slater working at the back of No. 59 had heard – although he had not reported this to the police until three days later. Mrs Donald had hidden the body in the cupboard beneath the sink, with the head in the cinder-box. She had calmly ironed her daughter's dresses and laid them out for her. She had then accompanied her to the Beach Pavilion and home again.

In the wee small hours of the Saturday morning, Mrs Donald

had padded across the kitchen floor to the cupboard. She had removed the body, thrust it into the sack and then dumped it in the deserted lobby. Edinburgh lawyer, William Roughead (1870–1952), Writer to the Signet, was a collector and author of murder cases and he attended the trial. Indeed, he was present at every major murder trial in Edinburgh over a period of sixty years. He believed that Helen and 'Coconut' had met, by fatal chance, at the Donalds' door. The child, he speculated, had roused the woman's fury, either by kicking the door, sticking out her tongue or mocking her in some way. Or it may have been simply a case of envy and bottled-up anger that turned the good-living, churchgoing house-wife into a killer.

When Mr Priestly was asked if his wife was on friendly terms with their downstairs neighbour, he told the court they had not spoken for five years. Mrs Priestly said it was four years. 'I ignored her. I did not like her,' she said. In her statement to the police, Mrs Donald, who described Helen as a 'nice quiet girlie', said relations had been strained because she had not taken Mrs Priestly's side in her row with a third-floor neighbour over a water leak. At one time, Helen and Jeannie Donald had been playmates. They had played with balls and dolls and sometimes they had danced in their frocks. On one occasion, they had fallen out and Jeannie had hit the younger girl and she had been warned not to do it again by her own mother.

Mrs Priestly had been left a small legacy and had bought their music-loving daughter a piano on her eighth birthday. They hired a music-teacher to give Helen private tuition at home. Whether this widened the rift between Mrs Priestly and Mrs Donald, who also wanted the very best for her only child, we do not know.

Mrs Donald's self-imposed silence, during the trial, had led to much speculation and innuendo but her side of the story was never made public. However, according to William Roughead's biographer, Richard Whittington-Egan, Lord Aitchison after-wards confided to Roughead that she had confessed her guilt.

The 'Aberdeen Sack Murder' has its place in the annals of crime because of Mrs Donald's final savage act – an outrage that had never before been known to have been committed by a woman – and her conviction, on circumstantial evidence, through forensic science.

Mrs Donald, whose roots were in Royal Deeside, met her ex-soldier husband while working in Banchory. She was a hotel cook – he was a hairdresser from Banff. She was released from jail on special licence on 26 June 1944. On the final day of her trial Mrs Donald's fate had filled columns in the Aberdeen press. But, on her release from Duke Street Prison, the world was at war. It was the Allied progress following the D-day landings in Normandy that occupied people's hearts and minds and, for the war-weary public, Mrs Donald's crime became an uneasy memory.

Helen Priestly was quietly buried in Allenvale Cemetery, over-looking the River Dee in Aberdeen, the day before the Donalds were arrested. Wreaths were sent by King Street School and Albion Street Sunday School. But she was not allowed to rest in peace. In the search for forensic clues, her body was exhumed on the evening of 30 May, six weeks after her murder, for samples of her hair to be taken. Because of this exhumation, a rule was introduced in Aberdeen that, in future cases of sudden death in suspicious circumstances, samples of hair, skin and fingernails must be taken before the funeral. (Curiously, this was done nineteen years before DNA was discovered!)

Helen's grave lies under a tree close by the east gate of the cemetery. The tombstone, which was erected by public subscription, bears a poignant epitaph:

> Grant that her little life
> So short here
> May unfold itself in thy sight.

5

LAST WOMAN TO HANG IN ABERDEEN

In the condemned cell on the morning of her execution in October 1830, Kate Humphrey wrung her bony hands and groaned, 'Oh, it's a sair thing to wash for the gibbet but I hope I will be washed in the blood of the Redeemer.' Mrs Humphrey, born Catherine Davidson at Keith Hall, near Inverurie, had murdered her sleeping husband by pouring the contents of a phial of vitriol (sulphuric acid) down his gaping throat. James Humphrey, a flesher and former dragoon with an English regiment, writhed in agony. 'I'm burned! I'm gone! I'm roasted!' he cried, as Kate tried to calm him by assuring him he must have taken 'bad drink'. He gasped, 'Oh, woman, woman, whatever I have gotten, it was in my own house. You have tried to do this often and you have done it now.' The bedclothes had scorch marks and a child, who put its lips to a glass standing on a table, cried out that it had been burnt. A servant spotted that there were three glasses on the table, yet, when her master retired for the night, there had only been two. A phial, which had previously contained three or four teaspoonfuls of oil of vitriol, was nearly empty. A small measure of vitriol added to water provided the working classes with a citrus-like drink.

A doctor could do little for Humphrey who, with his dying breath, absolved his wife of any crime. But, at the Autumn Circuit in 1830, the all-male jury would not be swayed. Lord Mackenzie sentenced her to death and ordered her body to be given to the anatomists. 'You will appear before God stained with the blood of a murdered husband,' he thundered. On the eve of her execution,

Mrs Humphrey, who accused her husband of being unfaithful, confessed her guilt, claiming that jealousy and malice had led her to commit murder.

The couple kept a public house in the Bowl Road, the ancient 'Bool-gait', which led eastwards from Park Street to the Links. In the year Kate Humphrey was hanged, the Police Commissioners agreed to change its name to Albion Street in the hope that it would alter the notorious character of the district. The Humphreys quarrelled constantly in front of friends and servants. During one blazing row, Humphrey tilted his throat and said to his razor-toting wife, 'There, do it now – for you will do it sometime!' He also made a chilling prediction that she would end her days 'looking down Marischal Street', a local euphemism for being hanged in the Castlegate. On Friday 8 October 1830, Kate, dressed entirely in black, was led, on the arms of her jailers, from the East Prison to the scaffold. But first she addressed the Lord Provost and magistrates in the courthouse. Drink, she told them, had been her downfall and she pleaded with them to weed out taverns with a bad reputation. (Her warnings appear to have gone unheeded. Seven years later, there was one public house for every eleven families living in the parish of Greyfriars.) Kate was close to fainting on the scaffold and did not raise her eyes to look at the huge crowd. But she found the courage to drop her handkerchief as a signal to John Scott, the city's new hangman. Her last words were, 'Oh, my God . . .'.

Kate Humphrey was the last woman to be hanged in Aberdeen. Her final days, according to a reporter, were tortured by the memory of being at the execution of Jean Craig, a habitual thief, in Aberdeen on 25 July 1784. Craig was sentenced to death for stealing cloth from a bleachfield at Huntly. At that time, it had been customary for the hangman to toss the rope he had used into the crowd and, following Craig's hanging, Kate Humphrey claimed to have been struck on the breast by the knot of the hangman's rope.

6

WALK TO THE GIBBET

1963

The tragic love affair of Harry Burnett and Margaret Guyan was doomed from the start. It destroyed the two men in her life. One was blasted at point-blank range by a shotgun and the other kept a date with the hangman. The young, star-crossed lovers first met in December 1962 when Margaret landed a job as a fish worker with J R Stephen, fish merchants in Torry, Aberdeen. Henry John Burnett (21) was attracted to the new employee and the feeling was mutual. But he was a former borstal boy, hot-headed with mental problems and a violent streak. In 1961 he had attempted suicide by swallowing sleeping tablets after a broken romance. And Margaret Guyan (25) was a married woman with two children, whose husband, Tommy, a merchant seaman, was away on the high seas. Margaret Henderson had married the affable Tommy Guyan (27) on 2 February 1957 and they went to live with her grandmother, Mrs Annie Henderson, who had been responsible for bringing up Margaret and her sister since they were babies. The newly-weds shared the comfortable middle-floor flat in Jackson Terrace, a twin row of granite houses tucked behind Urquhart Road, just round the corner from the house where Helen Priestly had been murdered. No. 14 Jackson Terrace overlooks Urquhart Lane, a road that follows the route of the former road to the gibbet on Gallow Hill.

In September 1958, the Guyans had a son and, in 1961, Margaret had another son but her husband was not the child's father. There were upsets and quarrels but Tommy, who was away at sea for long spells, continued to support his family. Margaret consulted a solicitor about a divorce but her husband wouldn't hear of it. While Tommy was at sea, Margaret and Harry Burnett lived as man and wife and they eventually rented a room from the occupant of a flat at 40 Skene Terrace in the city centre. Burnett had never seen Tommy Guyan, other than in a family snapshot. But his love for Margaret turned to jealousy on the last day of May 1963 when they heard Tommy had returned to port and Margaret said she was going back to her husband. Burnett locked the door of their room to try to prevent Margaret from leaving. In the subsequent commotion, their landlord persuaded Burnett to unlock the door and he then fled downstairs and into the street. Margaret, her neck bleeding from a knife wound inflicted by her lover, slumped into her rescuer's arms. Luckily, she was not badly hurt and she set off for Jackson Terrace to warn her husband.

Meanwhile, Burnett went to see his elder brother, Frank (29) at his work. He told him he had injured Margaret during a quarrel and Frank advised him to go to the police. Burnett agreed – at first. But revenge on Tommy Guyan was uppermost in his mind and he was given a lift by an old school chum to Frank's home in Bridge of Don. He failed to persuade his sister-in-law, Susie, to let him borrow her husband's double-barrelled shotgun. Frank had given her strict instructions not to lend the gun to anyone unless he was present. While Susie was distracted, Burnett forced open the cupboard where the gun was kept and removed the weapon and a handful of cartridges. He slipped out of the house and headed for the nearest bus stop.

Early that evening, 31 May, Tommy Guyan sat watching television in the living room at 14 Jackson Terrace with his wife. Mrs Annie Henderson sat in a chair with Margaret's infant son on her knee. Also there was a family friend, Georgina Cattanach. The programme was Gerry Anderson's *Fireball XL5*, a children's puppet drama. Suddenly the door burst open and Burnett, brandishing the shotgun, barged in. Tommy Guyan jumped to his feet. He asked Burnett who he was but he didn't get an answer. Burnett fired the gun and Tommy took the full force of the blast in his face. The force of the explosion knocked Mrs Henderson off the chair. She was struck in the shoulder but she was not seriously hurt. Pellets from the shotgun's cartridges scarred the floor, peppered a window and dented a gas heater. (I saw the marks when I was invited into the flat by the family.)

Before hustling Margaret out of the death flat, the killer calmly reloaded the gun and told her that, unless she came with him, he would shoot everybody. Schoolboy David Cousins (13), who lived with his grandparents in the flat upstairs, was confronted by Burnett on the stairs. Burnett pointed the gun at the boy and told him to get out of the way. A woman told the boy to phone for the police. Burnett had one hand around Margaret's waist and the gun in the other as he forced her up Urquhart Lane.

Blood and granite intermingled in Jackson Terrace that tragic summer evening in 1963. On the wall of a house next to King Street School, there is a variant of the family motto of the founder of the Marischal College. The inscription reads, 'Ne'er ye mind fut fowk say; bit dee ye weel an' lat them say'. The fifth Earl Marischal, George Keith (1553–1623), incurred bitter resentment when he endowed his new university with revenues from former monasteries. His contemptuous retort 'They have said; what they say? Let them say!' was adopted as the college motto. At the south-east corner, where No. 14 abuts on to Urquhart Lane, the body of Burnett's victim lay on the floor, the left side of his face shattered. By now Burnett and Margaret had reached the forecourt of James G Mutch (Motors) Limited, on the brow of Seaforth Road, at its junction with Erroll Street, a few steps from the Gallow Hill. As a petrol pump attendant filled up John Irvine's car, Burnett and Margaret approached. Burnett brandished the shotgun and demanded, 'Is this your car, pal?' When Irvine (25) said it was, the gunman told him, 'Okay. I'll take it now.' When Irvine tried deflate the tyres at the back of his car, Burnett pointed the gun at him and threatened him, saying, 'I've killed once – I'll kill again!' He then jumped into the driver's seat, with the gun across his knees and his hostage beside him. Irvine phoned the police as soon as the car had sped off.

As the getaway car headed north on the main Aberdeen to Peterhead road, Burnett made a bizarre request. He proposed marriage to Margaret and she accepted. Aberdeen City Police alerted police forces in north-east Scotland and road blocks were set up. The stolen car was intercepted at Ellon, Aberdeenshire, by a squad car from Peterhead. Burnett surrendered to Constable James Reaper, saying, 'It's me you want.'

Sergeant Ferguson Davidson (42) was on patrol-car duty when he received instructions on his radio to go to 14 Jackson Terrace. He was acting on the 999 call made by David Cousins. On the stairs leading to the flat, police and CID found two spent cartridges and, in the lobby of the flat, two fragments of bone. Sergeant Davidson was met by two women, Mrs Henderson and Georgina Cattanach, both of whom were hysterical. Tommy Guyan was lying on the living room floor. Mrs Henderson said to him, 'He did nothing to get that.' Burnett, she told him, had shot Guyan with a 'long gun'.

Detective Inspector Robert 'Paddy' Bell was in the yard at the city police HQ in Lodge Walk when the police car carrying Burnett and Margaret Guyan swept under the granite archway. Soon afterwards, a second car arrived. On the back seat was the murder weapon. When Detective Chief Inspector Harry Halcrow charged Burnett with murder, the accused replied, 'I gave him both barrels. He must be dead.'

Harry Burnett went on trial for his life at a sitting of the High Court in Aberdeen on Tuesday 23 July 1963. Queues for places in the public area of the court began at 7.15 a.m. The pavement outside Aberdeen Sheriff Court was clogged by people hoping to get a seat. (A few of them clutched newspapers that carried lurid details of the rich and famous at the Dr Stephen Ward vice trial which had opened at the Old Bailey. The notorious Christine Keeler and Mandy Rice Davies were witnesses and Christine's taxi would later be pelted with eggs and tomatoes.)

After the judge, Lord Wheatley, had arrived at the bench, preceded by a mace-bearer, a trapdoor opened in the well of the court and Burnett was led up to the dock from the cells. The fair-haired accused, relaxed and showing little signs of emotion, was dressed in a dark jacket, with black trousers and an open-necked pastel blue cotton shirt. Burnett denied capital murder and two assault charges – one of assaulting Margaret Guyan with a knife and the other of assaulting motorist John Irvine and robbing him of his car at gun point. Dr Robert Taylor QC, the defence counsel, lodged a special defence of insanity at the outset. Burnett smiled at some witnesses and even gave the 'thumbs up' sign of encouragement to his sister-in-law, Mrs Susie Burnett. But there was high drama during the hearing of police evidence when the dead man's mother, Mrs Jeannie Guyan, shouted in fury as her son's bloodstained shirt was held up for identification.

On the second day of the trial, Burnett's mood changed. When his mother, Mrs Matilda Burnett (52), was led to the witness box, Burnett frowned. Then, as the mother of seven was asked about her son's school background, she began to cry and Burnett snapped. Two truncheon-carrying, white-gloved policemen, sitting on either side of Burnett in the dock, grabbed him. He struggled to get free and shouted at Lord Wheatley, 'Tak' her oot!' Mrs Burnett stretched out a trembling hand and sobbed, 'Henry, it's okay – it's okay, my loon. I'm okay.' In the dock, Burnett slumped back in his seat and wept.

Later, when his mother again broke down, Burnett shouted, 'She's had enough, hasn't she?' Then he turned to a detective sitting behind him and said, 'She can't help being shaky.' Lord Wheatley told the pale-faced woman, 'Mrs Burnett, you understand you have been brought here as a witness by your son's legal advisers – presumably to help your son's interests. If you look at it from that point of view, perhaps you can be more composed.' Mrs Burnett refused the offer of a seat but sipped water as she told, in a low voice, of her son's troubled boyhood, of how he had played truant from school, of how he had threatened his sister with a knife and of his suicide bid. She admitted being frightened of him when he flew into a rage but, as she left the box, Mrs Burnett smiled at her son and he smiled back.

Burnett's father, Henry (62), said his son 'used to take awful turns'. 'He went kinda mad. He was not responsible for what he would do. You didn't know what to expect next. His face was white and his eyes staring in his head.' The boy had been all right until he had had an accident when he was twelve-years-old. But, in cross-examination with Mr W R Grieve QC, advocate-depute prosecuting, Burnett senior agreed that his son had injured his legs not his head.

The jury of ten women and five men heard tell of the accused man's state of mind. One witness said that Burnett had voluntarily entered Kingseat Hospital after his suicide attempt in 1961 but had then discharged himself against medical advice. Dr Ian Lowit (42), consultant psychiatrist at Aberdeen Sick Children's Hospital, had first seen Burnett in the casualty department at Aberdeen Royal Infirmary, Woolmanhill, after he had tried to kill himself with a drug overdose. 'My diagnosis at that time was that he was a psychopath but he was also depressed and in need of treatment.' Dr Taylor, defending, asked, 'Did you consider him as certifiable?' Dr Lowit said, 'If he had not entered as a voluntary patient, I would have certified him.'

Dr Lowit, who had been instructed on behalf of the Crown to examine Burnett at Aberdeen's Craiginches Prison, three days after the shooting, added that it was likely the prisoner had suffered an injury to his brain at an early age. Dr Taylor asked, 'Is he suffering from a mental disorder?' to which Dr Lowit, 'He is suffering from psychopathy which is a mental disorder recognised under the new Mental Health Act.' Lowit believed that Burnett was not capable of assessing the consequences of his acts. When cross-examined by Mr Grieve and asked what psychopathy meant, Dr Lowit said, 'It is a condition in which there is instability of temperament by reason of which the patient injures himself or society on repeated occasions.' For clarification, Mr Grieve asked, 'It means really soul-sick?' Dr Lowit agreed that it did. Dr Lowit told Mr Grieve that, although he had no evidence that Burnett's brain had been injured when he was young, he did think that Burnett had been of unsound mind when he attacked Mrs Guyan and shot her husband. Mr Grieve asked Dr Lowit, 'But not when he had threatened to shoot the man with the car?' and the doctor replied, 'I would not be prepared to pass an opinion on that.'

Mr Grieve then asked, 'What is the basis that he was of unsound mind when he cut Mrs Guyan's throat with a knife?' Dr Lowit replied that, throughout his life, Burnett had committed similar acts. He had threatened his mother and sister with a knife. He had attempted suicide and then discharged himself from hospital against medical advice. 'His whole life is comprised of impulsive unconsidered acts,' added Dr Lowit. 'Burnett,' he said, 'had a fear of throttling people and had sought medical advice because of that fear. I believe him to be insane insofar as he was incapable of considering the consequences of these acts.'

Neurologist Dr John Gaylor (59), a lecturer at Glasgow University, told the court that electric brainwave tests on Burnett had indicated that there was a tendency towards irritability of the brain at a particular point. He thought Burnett was insane at the time of the shooting and that he required institutional care.

Mr Grieve, addressing the jury, referred to the charges as 'the tragic three-act drama of 31 May', played out against the sordid background of a sailor's unfaithful wife and her lover who could not bear to see her favour being given to anybody but himself. He said Burnett's actions had been deliberate and it had been his intention to kill Thomas Guyan. The accused went to Jackson Terrace with a loaded shotgun, with the safety catch off, pointed it at

Guyan and pulled the trigger. The defence pleaded that, if the special defence of insanity was not sustained, the accused was suffering from diminished responsibility.

Lord Wheatley, in his two-hour summing-up on the last day of the three-day trial, said that Margaret Guyan might have been described as a 'femme fatale' or a somewhat fickle and immoral young woman. But her morals were not an issue. The jurors were to be concerned only about whether or not she made a credible witness. He suggested that the jury might think it had been established beyond doubt that jealousy was the motive. If the Crown had proved its case in regard to all three charges, they must then consider the special defence of insanity. In which case, they must take the evidence as a whole into account and not just the medical evidence.

The jury took twenty-five minutes to find Burnett guilty on all the three charges. Their finding was unanimous on the two assault charges and by a majority on the capital murder charge. Burnett barely flinched when the verdict was given. His sister, Mary, who was sitting between their father and their brother, Frank, wept. Mary leapt to her feet as the judge solemnly sentenced Burnett to death. 'Oh, no!', she shouted. 'They canna do that tae him.' She then indicated that Margaret Guyan should have been in the dock not her brother. The distraught girl was comforted by Frank as he led her and their father out of the courtroom. On the bench, Lord Wheatley brushed the black cap against his forehead as he pronounced doom. The execution date was fixed for Thursday 15 August.

After giving her evidence, Margaret Guyan went into hiding with reporters from a national newspaper. But, in an earlier interview, she told me she still stood by Burnett. 'I'm sorry for what has happened – but I love Harry.' But, after he was sentenced, Burnett did not mention Margaret's name when he spoke to his brother, Frank, in a cell below the court. 'He just threw his arms around me and wept,' said Frank. He said, 'I want to die – to put an end to all this.' Even as defence lawyers, surprised by the verdict, launched a special plea of clemency, the families of the condemned man and his victim got together to campaign for a reprieve. Twenty-four hours after his brother was sentenced to hang, Frank Burnett disclosed the contents of a letter written by his brother while he was still an untried prisoner in Craiginches. The letter, penned on official yellow, blue-lined stationery, was addressed to Frank and his wife, Susie. It read:

Dear Frank and Susie,

Just a few lines to let you know I am alright. As well as can be expected anyway. I am sorry for taking the gun and causing trouble for you and Susie but you know how quick-tempered I am. I will be here for a while yet so I was wondering if you would take up some comics for me as I am locked up most of the time. I know you will all blame Margaret. But please don't as she had no idea about what I was going to do. In fact I didn't know myself until I had done it. Well, Frank, Margaret still loves me so I think that means more to me than anything else could. I don't know what will happen but I think you have as good an idea as me. Hoping you will come up on Monday.

Love,

Henry

But Burnett's affections for Margaret had changed by the time Frank and his sister, Mary, became the first people to visit him in the condemned cell. He told them, 'I'm finished with Margaret. I don't want to see her. It's all over between us.' In the following week, Margaret received hate mail at her home in Jackson Terrace. One crank threatened to blind her with acid.

Harry Burnett refused to appeal against his sentence but desperate efforts were made to save him from the gallows. These culminated in a dramatic plea by Aberdeen Lord Provost, John M. Graham, and magistrates on the eve of his execution. Their last-ditch plea to Scottish Secretary Michael Noble, who was staying at Banff during a fact-finding tour of the north-east, fell on deaf ears. Grampian Television had already scrapped plans to broadcast an edition of their crime series, *Mind Behind Murder*, which had been due to be aired on 14 August. The edition, entitled 'Mrs Donald', was an account of the Helen Priestly murder and the subsequent trial. The TV company took the decision because of Burnett's impending execution and the fact Mrs Donald was still living in Scotland.

At Craiginches Prison, which had not witnessed an execution since it was opened in 1891, joiners had completed work on the scaffold. Although the Scottish Office had sent the rope for the hanging, they later billed the city council for £10. The hangman had been chosen by magistrates from a list of six names, in alphabetical order, that had been submitted by the Scottish Office in Edinburgh. The name at the top of the list was the flamboyant Harry Allen, from Manchester.

Sunshine struggled through grey skies as a silent crowd of 200 men, women and a few children gathered outside the jail on the day of the execution. John Gibson staged a one-man protest against capital punishment, displaying sandwich boards bearing the messages 'Abolish Legal Murder' and 'Vengeance is Mine Sayeth The Lord'.

The night before, Burnett had downed a nip of whisky and had slept quite well. In the morning, he was offered another dram but refused, claiming that the one he had the previous night had been drugged. He had a mug of tea instead. The prisoner, dressed in a loose, open-necked shirt and blue trousers, walked into a room adjoining the execution chamber where he took part in a religious service with the prison chaplain, Rev. John Dickson, minister of St Fittick's Church, and Canon Charles Glennie of St Peter's Episcopal Church. Rev. Dickson, now living in retirement in Banchory, visited Burnett every day in the weeks leading up to the execution. He and the prison officers kept Burnett occupied with cards and dominoes. Burnett, Dickson said, had never meant to shoot Guyan. 'He didn't intend it to happen. He knew he had done it and was very, very sorry. He was very sincere and quite a decent lad at heart.' The prisoner's arms were pinned to his sides by a leather strap, while the leg strap was looped round his thighs. According to another eye-witness, Burnett 'trotted' into the execution chamber, escorted by Allen, the hangman, and his unnamed assistant. Two prison officers stood on either side of the trap as Rev. Dickson prayed. Two magistrates and the prison doctor were also there. The minister held out the silver cross of St John, a souvenir of a visit to Iona, as Burnett approached the 'drop'. Rev. Dickson said, 'He was looking at me all the time. I had the cross in my hand and I was within touching distance of him. His mind was made up and he didn't hesitate for a moment. He was a very brave lad.' The cross was the last thing Burnett saw before a white linen hood went over his head. On reaching the 'drop', the hangman's assistant tightened the leg strap. Hangman Allen flicked the noose over Burnett's head. His assistant stepped smartly out of the way as Allen pulled a lever. Burnett died instantly and without a sound. In the streets outside, the crowd fell silent. The clock on the prison belfry showed one minute past eight. From the time he entered the chamber to the moment the 'drop' fell, nine seconds had elapsed. Burnett, who was medically discharged from an army service corps after six months because he had been considered unfit for duty, had died like a soldier.

Two prison officers and the principal officer who had been with him in the condemned cell during those last days were distraught. Outside the jail, the crowd was told no notice would be posted on the gates. After a few hours, they dispersed reluctantly. Allen and his assistant later enjoyed a refreshment in the canteen at police headquarters at Lodge Walk. He told his hosts, 'That was a very easy job.' A year later, on 13 August 1964, Allen and Edinburgh-born hangman, Jock Stewart, executed murderers Peter Anthony Allen and Gwynne Owen Evans at Liverpool and

Manchester respectively – the last-ever hangings in the United Kingdom. Burnett also made Scottish criminal history as he was the last man to be hanged in Scotland.

Soon after the execution, Burnett's body was put in a coffin and, after a funeral service conducted by Rev. Dickson, he was carried by prison officers to a prepared grave behind Craiginches. He was buried behind the custom-built execution block which had been built the previous year. The building is now an administration block. The square 'pit', into which his body dropped when the fatal trap was sprung, now serves as a stationery store. In the past, it was customary to hoist a black flag at the moment of execution and to display it for one hour at a conspicuous point in the prison. Like the tolling of the prison or church bell, the black flag has been confined to history.

Should Burnett have hanged? Three months after the execution, Professor W Malcolm Millar, of the Chair of Mental Health at Aberdeen University, said he might refuse to give evidence at future murder trials where the degree of responsibility was a main issue. He told the *Scottish Daily Mail* that he genuinely felt that, because of the differing views of human responsibility held by doctors and lawyers, he would do the prisoner more harm than good. His comments, which caused a stir in Scottish legal circles, were prompted by the reprieve of a condemned murderer in a case identical to that of Burnett's.

Two of the doctors who gave evidence at Burnett's trial were convinced that Burnett should not have hanged. Dr Ian Lowit told the *Mail* that, if he had the choice, he would never get involved in a similar case again under the present system. Dr John Gaylor revealed how he made a last-ditch bid to save Burnett's life while on holiday in Norway. He dictated an urgent medical memo on the case and asked the British Embassy in Oslo to relay it to the Scottish Secretary via the Foreign Office. 'I felt most strongly that Burnett should not hang,' he said.

ABERDEEN'S LAST PUBLIC HANGING

Burnett's execution was the first to take place in Aberdeen for 106 years. Back then, in 1857, the Indian Mutiny was headline news – as was the sensational murder trial of Madeleine Smith, a wealthy Glasgow architect's daughter, who was acquitted of poisoning her secret lover.

On 21 October of that year, John Booth, a hawker, was hanged in public for stabbing his mother-in-law, Jean Barclay, as she protected his flighty wife during a domestic feud in Oldmeldrum, Aberdeenshire. Booth walked directly to the scaffold from an open window on the first floor of the burgh courtroom in Castle Street and into the waiting arms of the London hangman William Calcraft, who had been savagely hissed by the crowd of 2,000 when he appeared on the scaffold. The bushy-bearded Calcraft was well known to the Aberdeen mob. In previous years he had hanged George Christie, the Kittybrewster murderer, and John Robb, who had murdered and raped an old woman in her cottage at Auchterless, Aberdeenshire, after climbing down the chimney.

Booth met his fate stoically. After he was cut down, he was interred beside Christie and Robb in the precincts of the East Jail, which stood behind the Aberdeen Tolbooth museum. (Seven years after Booth's execution Calcraft recommended Aberdeen druggist John Jamieson for the job of burgh hangman, subject to him getting lessons from the master!) Booth was the last person to be publicly hanged in Aberdeen. Scotland's last public execution took place in Dumfries on 12 May 1868 when Yorkshireman Tommy Askern dispatched Robert Smith (19), a farmhand, for murder, rape and robbery. His victim was ten-year-old Thomasina Scott, whom he lured into a wood near the village of Cummertrees. Britain's last public hanging took place a fortnight later when Calcraft, who had been too busy to travel to Dumfries, executed Michael Barrett for leading a Fenian raid on the Clerkenwell House of Detention in London, during which twelve people were killed in an explosion. Three days later, a new law was given royal approval, which meant that future executions could only take place within the privacy of the prison walls. Scotland's first-ever private execution took place at Perth on 4 October 1870 when Calcraft hanged George Chalmers, a native of Fraserburgh, Aberdeenshire, for the brutal murder of a tollkeeper at Braco, Perthshire.

7

SCREAMS IN TORRY

1945

A cold finger of wind ruffled the dark, oily water of Aberdeen docks as the elderly beachcomber sifted through the scattered ships' debris that had washed ashore at Torry, on the south side of the navigation channel. Alexander King (74) had just reached a point about 100 yards east of the junction of Greyhope Road and St Fittick's Road, when he froze. His eyes were fixed on a pale-coloured object which lay like some obscene marine creature below the high-water mark, among the seaweed-coated pebbles and rocks. It was a human left forearm with the hand still attached. The retired cooper hastily abandoned collecting driftwood and scrambled up the bank to raise the alarm. One report would later claim that he had carried the severed limb to a police box in Victoria Road, at the Torry side of the Victoria Bridge.

The local newspaper, the *Evening Express* – priced 1½d and reduced to tabloid size, with just eight pages, because of post-war newsprint rationing – ran a front-page story later that day, Wednesday 12 December 1945, with the blood-chilling headline

GRIM FIND ON ABERDEEN FORESHORE –
Sawn-off Arm and Hand: Foul Play Suspected

Police surgeon Dr Robert Richards, who had examined the Urquhart Road murder victim, Helen Priestly, in 1934, deduced that a saw with fine teeth had been used and that the direction of the saw had been changed in the process. He reported that it was

73

likely that the limb belonged to a female of about eighteen years of age who probably been alive three days earlier. Although the back of the hand had been eaten by crabs, it appeared that the limb had only been in the water for a short time. These deductions would prove remarkably accurate. It seemed that the dead teenager had smoked because the fingers, arched with rigor mortis, were nicotine stained. A police spokesman said that, although the 'disarticulation was a very neat piece of work', it was 'not necessarily the work of a medical man'. Mutilation by a ship's propeller was discounted. Detectives found something else of interest. A length of binder twine, tied in a granny knot, was bound loosely round the wrist. The loop had probably contained a weight, perhaps a heavy stone, which had slipped out by accident when it was dumped in the water. A granny knot resembles a reef knot but is less reliable.

On the day of the grim discovery, uniformed policemen in helmets, waterproofs and rubber boots and wielding 'graips' – garden forks – began scouring the southern foreshore. Tons of rocks, pebbles and seaweed were turned over in the hunt for clues. In days to come, policemen swapped their regulation headgear for flat caps and resembled inshore fishermen as they took to the water. A small fleet of rowboats and yawls worked inshore with grappling irons in the hope of finding body parts. A press photo by Marshall Gloyer captured the moment.

Detective Superintendent John Westland, who had interviewed the child-murderer Jeannie Donald, led the inquiry and, within four hours of the arm being discovered, his men had identified the murdered girl. She was named as Elizabeth Ann Craig or Hadden – known to her friends as Betty – whose widowed mother lived at 9 Manor Walk in the Middlefield district of Aberdeen. She had been a few days short of her eighteenth birthday. The police broke the news to Mrs Kate Hadden (38), widow of Albert Hadden who had died two years ago.

The early breakthrough, described as a 'brilliant start' by the

74

local press, was due to the police having taken fingerprints of Betty Hadden's hand. By a stroke of luck her 'dabs' were on a file at police headquarters as she had been arrested on some minor offence. They also issued photos to reporters. They show a sulky teenager, her brunette hair worn at shoulder length. She is dressed in an open-necked blouse and a jacket with large checks. Since leaving school, Betty had had a number of mundane jobs – a hotel scullery maid and a kitchen maid and a restaurant waitress – but she had failed to hold down any of them for any length of time. Although most of her work had been in the catering trade, she had also worked at Broadford Works, a city textile mill, and, at one point, she had also been employed as an agricultural worker. Her last job was gutting fish. Her mother admitted that her daughter had only stuck at her last two jobs for three days. Betty's restless nature had tempted her to seek excitement and easy money in seedy back-street pubs and dance halls. She had probably found what she was looking for as scrutiny of her left hand revealed no obvious indications of hard work.

Her disappearance sparked off the most prolonged and intensive probe in the city force's history but it was hampered by the reluctance of male associates of the girl to come forward with information. Four months had passed since VJ Day, which heralded the surrender of Imperial Japan and the end of the Second World War, but it seemed that the public hadn't had enough blood-letting. In Glasgow, 100 red-haired men were checked as police hunted a gunman who had killed a woman and a boy porter at Pollokshields East railway station. (Charles Templeman Brown was sentenced to hang for these crimes but was reprieved. He died in a car crash in 1960.) In Europe, the shrunken head of a Polish inmate at Buchenwald was exhibited at the Nazi war criminal trial at Nuremberg. And in Hameln, the setting for Robert Browning's poem about the Pied Piper, Josef Kramer, the Beast of Belsen, and three women, including Irma Grese (21), who lashed prisoners to death with a whip, were among a group of guards from the notorious concentration camp executed by British hangman Albert Pierrepoint.

Aberdonians lived in the most frequently bombed city in Scotland during the war. They were keen to carry on their favourite wartime recreation – visiting the cinema. For economic reasons, the city had lost three cinemas, the Star, the Globe and the King's, but still boasted sixteen (seventeen, if you include His Majesty's Theatre which showed films when there were no live productions). To get away from the horror of the Betty Hadden murder and Nazi death camps, film fans queued to be enchanted by a sentimental and glossy musical from the Hollywood dream merchants, for as little as 9d a ticket. But the silver screen could also terrify its audiences. As the mystery of the missing teenager deepened, the Belmont offered patrons, *Seven Doors to Death*, while, round the corner in Union Street, the Queen's Cinema was showing *I Love a Good Mystery*. Fans seeking more chills flocked to *Dead of Night*, the classic British supernatural thriller, which was being screened at the Picture House.

But, as filmgoers filed out of the warm picture palaces into a drab December night with the national anthem echoing in their ears, they no doubt asked themselves, 'What has befallen Betty Hadden?' There was no doubt she had been done to death but who was the culprit and where and when did the brutal murder take place? Daily bulletins calling for witnesses to come forward were issued to the press. In their investigations, police took into account the possibilities that Betty's dismembered limb could have been washed in from the sea or carried down the River Dee.

Each dawn, the rubber-booted bobbies resumed their search of the foreshore, extending it from the navigation channel to Girdleness Lighthouse and on to the rocky Bay of Nigg, about two miles away, to the south. Upstream from the channel, search parties combed the banks of the Dee, while their colleagues concentrated on the sea beach which stretched from Footdee, across the channel, to the River Don in the north. The hunt extended into Balnagask golf course, south of Greyhope Road. The golf course had lain unused since the start of the war and it was dotted with ugly red-brick billets and bunkers which had housed troops. In the not-too-distant future these would be occupied by squatters with no homes of their own. Nearby allotments were also dug up in the search. In the coming weeks, hundreds of miles of the east coast of Scotland, from John o' Groats to Berwick, were scoured by other police forces. No stone or tangle of seaweed was left unturned to find the remains of Betty Hadden. Checks were made on ships tied up in dock and shipping agents and owners made requests for onboard searches to be done by the crews of vessels that had already sailed. Sailors and fishermen were asked if they had seen the missing girl. Ships, known to have been in Aberdeen on the day and night before the grisly discovery of Betty's limb, were boarded by police at their next port of call.

In Aberdeen, the police intensified their search for anyone who had spoken to Betty or seen her. As information came in, they were able to fit some of the missing pieces of the jigsaw together. On Friday 7 December, she had been in Torry where she visited relatives. On the following Monday, a girl who was about to board a tram in Castle Street, spotted her arm-in-arm with two sailors. She recognised Betty from the photograph issued to the public. Around forty minutes later, she was again seen in Castle Street. This time she was walking with four other girls on the pavement outside the Town House. But it was later established that she had not been in their company after all. The police had less luck in tracing a fifteen-year-old youth who had been seen in her company on two separate occasions. The youth had acted as a go-between, carrying a note from Betty to a friend of hers in a city dance hall. Step by step the police built up a picture of Betty's last movements, as she wandered the East End of the city at all hours of the day and night. Her mother last saw her waif-like daughter more than ten days before the murder hunt had begun but she wasn't unduly worried by this as it had not been the first time her daughter had left home.

A *Scottish Daily Express* reporter compared the gruesome find with the infamous Dr Buck Ruxton case of 1935. A murder hunt had been launched after the grim discovery of pieces of two women's bodies in a gully near Moffat in Dumfriesshire. The remains were those of the doctor's missing wife and her maid. Ruxton, a Parsee, of Lancaster, was found guilty of murder and he was hanged at Strangeways on 12 May 1936. Professor (later Sir) Sydney Smith, of Edinburgh University, was among the hundred or so witnesses to give evidence for the Crown at the Ruxton trial. He estimated that it had taken Ruxton eight hours to dismember and mutilate the two bodies.

During the Hadden investigation, Professor Smith came to Aberdeen to conduct the oral examinations of fourth-year students at the medical school. It was too good an opportunity for the police to miss. Professor Smith agreed to help police surgeon Dr Richards in a re-examination of Betty's pitiful remains. It was the first time they had worked together since the Urquhart Road murder. Professor Smith confirmed the finding of Dr Richards and forensic experts at Aberdeen University that the arm had been in the water for no more than twenty-four hours. This meant that the limb must have been dumped on the night of Tuesday 11 December. It was agreed that both a saw and knife had been used to dismember the arm. The size of the saw and the pressure that the killer had exerted could be determined from the marks it made on the bone and from the point at which the bone had splintered. By reconstructing the body's dismemberment, the noted surgeon, Sir John Learmonth, was able to prove the actual position in which Betty's corpse had been lying when the killer had sawn off her forearm. The next step was to see if it was possible to ascertain whether the limb been dumped in the water at sea or thrown there from the land.

To find the answer, an ingenious experiment was carried out by police with help from marine scientists. The foreleg of a pig, doubling as the severed arm, was dropped into the water at different spots around the estuary, harbour and river to see where it would land. It was the pig's leg from the Torry side that floated ashore in the vicinity of the spot where the gruesome discovery was made on 12 December and the conclusion was that Betty's limb had been thrown in the water from the Torry shore. But where the murder and amputation had taken place remained a deep mystery. A huge mass of material collected on the Torry shore – scraps of cloth, bits of metal, anything that might hold a clue – was checked and labelled by detectives. A sample of the twine that had been knotted round Betty's forearm was examined by Dr H S Holden at the police laboratory at Nottingham. His analysis revealed that it was only common binder twine of the kind used by farmers and also by many others.

A few days after Professor Sydney Smith returned to Edinburgh, detectives were able to narrow down Hadden's movements before her murder. A woman, who was a casual acquaintance of Betty, had met her in Park Street at lunch-time on Tuesday afternoon. Betty had asked her if she knew where she could get a night's lodgings. The woman told Betty that she didn't and Betty left, saying that she thought she knew a woman in the George Street direction who would put her up. As she walked off, she called out, 'Cheerio!' The meeting took place twenty-one hours before elderly Alec King's search for driftwood was hastily cut short. That evening, Betty was said to have given three sailors the 'glad eye' in Market Street.

Despite the huge dragnet involving police from Aberdeen, Aberdeenshire, Kincardineshire and beyond, the murder probe seemed to falter. Hopes were raised and then dashed when a human leg thrown up near the storm-battered Bullers of Buchan, south of Peterhead, was identified as belonging to a male. Many such severed limbs had been washed up during the war. A storm, that battered the north-east coast, brought flooding to the Dee and Don valleys and with the rough weather came a dangerous reminder of the war. A mine, that had broken loose from its moorings at sea, drifted more than a mile up the River Ythan to land on the river bank opposite Tarty Farm, near Ellon, and had to be dismantled by the navy.

On Christmas Day 1945, Aberdeen CID issued the following dramatic statement regarding the murder mystery:

> Information to the police, during the past few days, has established that, about 2 a.m. on Wednesday 12 December, screams, described as being made by a female in terror, were heard by several people at different points in the Torry district. The points at which the screams were heard strongly suggest that they came from within Mansefield Road, Victoria Road, St Fittick's Road and the south side of the River Dee. If the person who screamed was not Betty Hadden, it is of vital importance that the police should learn who that person was.

Detectives believed the murder had taken place in Torry in the early hours of 12 December, probably between 2 a.m. and 5 a.m.. Police stepped up their house-to-house search in Old Torry and the surrounding neighbourhood. 'We shall go through Torry yard by yard,' promised their spokesman. They also wanted to trace the drivers or occupants of motor vehicles seen in the area during the early hours of that fateful morning. The Torry house-to-house check, I discovered, brought some welcome humour to a grisly subject. It was said the proud housewives of Old Torry gave their front doorsteps an extra scrub and their ornaments an extra dusting when they heard of the impending visit by the law. Police, who knocked on their doors, would inevitably be offered a cup of tea.

William Bruce, who was in the RAF during the war, told me of an amusing incident on the day plain-clothes police called at his parents' home in Baxter Street. His father, William Bruce senior, was sub postmaster of the post office at the corner of Baxter Street and Abbey Road. He had opened Torry's first official post office in 1920. During the house-to-house check, which involved searching lanes, back greens, gardens and hundreds of sheds, wash-houses and air-raid shelters, a policeman mounted the loft ladder at the Bruce home. There followed his heart-stopping cry, 'She's here – I've found her!' He then descended with a child's doll in his grasp. It belonged to William junior's wee sister, Sheena. 'The policeman had a sense of humour,' he laughed. 'But my mother wasn't so amused!'

A map of Torry had been divided into squares and, each day, a particular section was scoured. Dragging operations in the navigation channel were abandoned because of the spate in the Dee. The police re-enacted the mystery woman's screams in the night. A small group of their clerical staff and a policewoman volunteered. The females, escorted by officers, each took a turn in screaming at the top of their lungs. This was performed at the various points where the terrified cries were first heard. A young policeman was at hand with a hip flask to keep out the raw night air. After each high-pitched scream, there was a pause to judge the reaction of the sleeping folk of Old Torry. But not a single bedroom light was flicked on, not one lace curtain twitched. Even though the test had failed, the police were still determined to find out who screamed. 'This line of inquiry will be pursued until we get a satisfactory answer to the question,' commented a police spokesman. 'If the person who screamed was not Betty Hadden, whose screams were they?'

The first Hogmanay since the end of the war kept the bakers busy. 'It's been like the V Days all over again,' said an Aberdeen bakery manager. Bakers worked round the clock to deal with the bread queues. There were ten New Year's Day babies born in the city. But, as 1946 progressed, the murder hunt ran out of steam. Years later, Detective-Inspector Bill Spence described it as the most concentrated inquiry he had been on.

The case was filed under 'Unsolved'. Betty's arm was preserved in the anatomy department at the university. The late John Nicol, a former Assistant Chief Constable of Grampian Police, told me how he had produced the macabre object at a lecture he gave in

Aberdeen to legal and medical people. Talk had turned to the murder and the killer's method of amputation. Nicol gleefully recalled how the bottled arm was held up to the glare of the roof lights so that bow-tied guests could get a better look. The arm was disposed of some years ago and the terrified screams of Betty Hadden are now a faint, ghostly echo in time.

The place where her forearm was found would still be recognisable to the gum-booted bobbies who dug for clues on the Torry foreshore. The South Breakwater, the 'banana peerie' and the 'skate's nose' are enduring landmarks. Sadly, the hamlet of Old Torry, which was granted a royal charter in 1495, was sacrificed to North Sea oil in the early 1970s. Oil-industry support ships are now moored where fast air–sea rescue launches and Walrus seaplanes had been tied up during the war. The salmon fishers, who used to go about their business on the sickle of sandy beach and who always found time to point out to inquisitive schoolboys the difference between a bootlace and a pipe fish, have also departed. But the murder mystery lingers in the memory of an older generation.

Well might they wonder what happened to Betty Hadden. In a series on true crime in the *Scottish Sunday Express* in October 1955, journalist Peter Piper investigated the ten-year-old mystery. He concluded that many police officers were convinced that someone in Torry knew something that could lead to the solving of the mystery. Piper believed that Betty, shiftless and haphazard as she was, was not a 'pick-up girl' in the accepted sense of that phrase. Piper wrote:

> I feel convinced that, on the night of 11 December, she met someone ruthless and brutal and savage enough to attempt, by force, to overcome her. She fought against this man and died . . . And I believe, too, that this man lived in Torry or nearby or at least had access to some building there where he dismembered the body.

My own theory is that Betty Hadden was murdered and dismembered in Torry and her remains dumped in the channel. She probably knew her killer. I understand the police did have a suspect in mind but he is now beyond justice, having died some years ago.

8

BABY KILLER

1955

Time was running out for Robert James Boyle (24) in the condemned cell at Craiginches Prison. The cherubic-faced Boyle, a former chauffeur from Paisley, was under sentence of death for child murder in Aberdeen. He had been due to hang on 28 February 1956. But, because of an impending hearing at the Scottish Court of Criminal Appeal against his conviction, the execution had been postponed. The appeal was dismissed and, in five days' time, Boyle was due to keep a new date with the hangman.

Boyle's case made legal history. It was the first Scottish case, in modern times, to secure a conviction without a body. The body of the victim, his nine-day-old baby, was never found. The baby's mother was teenager Barbara Irvine, who first met Boyle at the Glasgow engineering firm where they worked. Irvine was an office worker and Boyle was a chauffeur. When they had become friendly in August 1954, he had told her he was single but he later confessed that he was married with three children. He added that he and his wife had separated and they were getting a divorce.

He gave Irvine an engagement ring and she understood they would eventually marry. In February 1955, Barbara told him she was pregnant with his child but she did not tell her parents. At the end of July, Boyle, who was by now working as a corporation bus-driver in Glasgow, quit his job and the couple moved to Aberdeen. It was decided they should stay there for a month, if not longer. Irvine's parents were unaware of their plan.

They lodged with Mr and Mrs Alexander Rilley in a tenement

flat at 1 Powis Crescent on the understanding that they would have to quit the flat at the end of September. During the months they were there, they lived as man and wife and Irvine was known as 'Mrs Boyle'. Boyle found a job with Aberdeen Corporation Transport Department and, on 26 August, Irvine, who was eighteen at the time, gave birth to a baby boy in Aberdeen Maternity Hospital. The baby was called Andrew Boyle. While Barbara was in hospital, Boyle had bought clothes and nappies for the child. But, when mother and child left hospital on 7 September, the baby didn't have a proper cot. He slept in a suitcase with the lid secured by string to a chair. A pillow served as a mattress and a folded blanket kept the baby warm.

On the day of the new baby's homecoming to Powis Crescent, the couple discussed moving on. Boyle wanted to go to Newcastle for work but Irvine said it was too far for such a young child to travel. By the following day, Thursday 8 September, they had still not decided where they would go next. Irvine would have preferred to move back to Glasgow but, if Boyle wanted her to accompany him to Newcastle, she would have the baby adopted. Boyle made a sinister remark as he went out. He told her there were other ways they could get rid of the baby. That afternoon, a health visitor called and Irvine told her she was going to Glasgow.

When Boyle returned home around 6 p.m., he suggested smothering the baby. Irvine would have none of it and he left. He went to a cafe and later watched a minor football match before returning to the flat. He waited until the Rilleys went out for the evening before rejoining Irvine at their digs. It looked like an ordinary domestic scene as Irvine sat knitting and her partner put on the fire. But their conversation was far from normal. He asked her if she could smother the child. 'No, I can't do it,' she told him. He claimed he wasn't the baby's father and volunteered to do it. She became upset and broke down. She then went into the bathroom to sponge her eyes. When she came back a few minutes later, their bedroom door was locked.

She tried to get into the room but Boyle called out to her to go away. On her return a few minutes later, the door was still locked. Irvine asked Boyle what he was doing and again he told her to go away. The baby was crying. She had the impression his cries were being stifled. Once again Irvine retreated to the bathroom where she stayed for about twenty minutes. She heard the bedroom door open and someone go out the front door. When she finally plucked up courage to enter the bedroom, the baby and Boyle had gone. Andrew's pillow lay at the foot of the bed. Also missing was her small wine-coloured shopping bag. A stricken Barbara Irvine was alone in the house as their landlady and her husband had not yet returned.

Meanwhile, the killer walked down George Street and headed for the docks, with the body in the shopping bag. Boyle tied a brick round the corpse's leg and, when he got to the harbour, he dumped the little body in Victoria Dock, opposite Commerce Street. Afterwards, Boyle caught a bus home. He appeared upset when he got back and a distraught Irvine sat crying, her head buried in her hands. Despite her growing fear of Boyle and a suspicion that he had done away with the baby, she spent the night with him in the bedroom. She had no money and no place to go. Next morning, they packed up and, after leaving behind a farewell note for the Rilleys, the couple left by train for Newcastle. Boyle had raised money for the fares by selling the fur coat he had bought Irvine while they were courting.

Boyle landed a job as a bus-driver in Newcastle but, at the end of October, he was arrested on a charge of neglecting his family in Paisley. He later appeared at Glasgow Sheriff Court and was sent to Barlinnie Jail. Barbara Irvine decided to return to her parents. She took a train north and her father met her at the railway station. Her father could tell something was wrong so she told him she had had a baby and that it had been adopted. Because the station was crowded, she did not want to upset her father by telling him what had really happened and it was only when they got home that she changed her story and claimed that the infant had been accidentally suffocated. Before he had gone to prison, Boyle had warned her never to tell anyone the truth.

Because of the weight of Barbara's suitcase, her father suspected that the baby's body might have been locked inside it. Wanting to avoid opening it himself, Mr Irvine reported his suspicions to Govan police. When Detective Constable Thomas Stewart arrived at the Irvines' house, Barbara's father handed him the keys to the suitcase. The police officer interviewed Barbara Irvine before examining and then unlocking the suitcase. In it, he found baby clothes, Boyle's clothing and some toiletries.

In November, Barbara went to Aberdeen with her father to register the baby as Andrew Irvine, with herself as the mother and the space for the father's name left blank. The birth certificate extract was handed to Detective Inspector Harry Halcrow, who later travelled to Glasgow with his colleague, Detective Inspector Robert Bell, to interview Boyle, who was then at the end of his month-long sentence. They later charged Boyle with murder. He told the Aberdeen detectives that Barbara had tried to smother the baby with the bedcover. 'I just finished the job with the pillow,' he said. He described how he put the body in the shopping bag and walked down to the harbour where he dropped it in the water. 'She was pleased I got rid of it,' he claimed. When he was taken back to Aberdeen, Boyle showed police the place where he had thrown the body. Although divers searched the bed of Victoria Dock for six-and-a-half hours it was never found.

Boyle's trial opened at the High Court in Aberdeen on 31 January 1956, as fierce blizzards swept the north-east. An army of snow ploughs fought to keep roads open as huge seas battered the coast. At the courthouse the judge, Lord Hill-Watson, inspected the traditional guard of honour, the Gordon Highlanders, indoors because of the inclement weather. Boyle, a dapper figure in black blazer, white shirt and blue-grey flannels, pleaded not guilty to suffocating the baby with a pillow. His defence counsel lodged a special plea, claiming that the baby had been killed by his mother. Barbara Irvine, smartly dressed in a fur coat and a tan hat with matching handbag, was the first prosecution witness.

The local *Evening Express* described how, in a tense cross-examination by defence counsel, Mr W I R Fraser QC, she was asked, 'Wasn't it you who murdered this baby?' Her reply rang out through the crowded yet hushed court, 'No, I did not kill the baby.' Irvine later claimed that the reason she had changed her story more than once was because she was frightened of Boyle and what he might have done to her. She said that, after Boyle had suggested that she smother the baby, she left the room. When she had returned from the bathroom, the door was locked but she had heard the baby crying as if from a far distance. 'I thought Boyle had something over the baby's mouth,' she told the court.

Policewoman Gladys Scott of Govan Police had interviewed Irvine at home on two occasions. On 30 October, Irvine, who was ill in bed, said that the baby had died in bed during the night of 8 September. She made the tragic discovery when she woke up. Boyle's involvement was not mentioned. But Scott visited Barbara again, two days later, to check some discrepancy in her statement. This time, Irvine told her that Boyle had smothered the child with a pillow on the evening of 8 September. Boyle told her he had disposed of the body where no one would find it – but he did not say where. The policewoman felt Irvine had been very confused when she had first interviewed her. However, when she called again, a more relaxed Irvine was able to give a much clearer statement.

Boyle, the only defence witness, went into the box and accused Irvine of the murder. The court listened as Boyle described how he had returned to 1 Powis Crescent on the evening of 8 September. Irvine had met him at the door and told him the baby was dead. 'I thought she had seen a ghost,' he said. She was pure white.' The child had been lying on the bed with the bedclothes and pillow over his face. Boyle claimed that he had tried to revive the baby but he was dead. 'Barbara Irvine killed the baby,' he said. 'I didn't do it.' In his summing-up at the end of the two-day trial, in which thirty witnesses gave evidence, Lord Hill-Watson said:

> This is one of these murder cases in which there is no halfway house. This is murder or nothing. If, on the Crown's evidence, you think that this man had a hand in putting a little life out of existence, it is your duty to return a verdict of guilty. If you are not satisfied – because you think that the girl is not truthful or that Boyle's evidence is true or that his evidence weakens hers – it is clearly your duty to acquit him.

But the jury of eight women and seven men did not believe Boyle's story. They found him guilty by a majority verdict. As the judge passed the death sentence, Barbara Irvine, sat expressionless, her eyes averted. She quickly left the court by a back door with her parents. A trapdoor in front of the dock opened and Boyle, escorted by two white-gloved policemen, hurried down the steps to the cells below. His next stop was the condemned cell at Craiginches Prison where he was due to hang on 28 February. His defending QC told reporters, 'We are considering an appeal.'

It was Aberdeen's first death sentence in nearly fifty years. Back in September 1907, Joseph Hume (24), an army deserter from Fort George, had been condemned to death, at the High Court in Aberdeen, for the murder of John Barclay Smith (48), a road contractor, working for Elgin County Council. The murder took place in the victim's home at Lhanbryde, Morayshire. Hume had repaid Smith's kind offer of work and shelter by battering his drunken host with a roadman's hammer before stealing money and Smith's gold watch. In Edinburgh, he had roused a pawnbroker's suspicions when he tried to pawn the watch.

However, it was decided that Hume would hang in Inverness and this angered local magistrates who wanted the execution foisted on to Aberdeen as that was where the sentence had been given. But, despite the magistrates protests and a public petition for a reprieve, Hume walked to the scaffold, borrowed from Glasgow, on 5 March 1908. Objections by residents around Inverness's Porterfield Prison meant that the bell remained silent, although the traditional black flag was hoisted to indicate the sentence had been carried out.

On the same day that Boyle was sentenced to die, a private bill to suspend the death penalty for five years was introduced by Sydney Silverman, Labour MP for Nelson and Colne. Meanwhile, Boyle's lawyers pressed ahead with an appeal but, at the hearing in Edinburgh on 22 February 1956, three judges, headed by Lord Thomson, the Lord Justice Clerk, agreed that there was ample evidence, from separate sources, to justify the verdict. Boyle's wife, who had sued for divorce on the eve of her husband's trial, attended the hearing accompanied by Boyle's uncle. The condemned man winked and nodded to the couple as he left the dock between two prison officers. A new date for his execution in Aberdeen was fixed for 10 March – a Saturday. Boyle's hopes now rested on his lawyers.

But, on Monday 5 March, the *Aberdeen Evening Express* splashed news of Boyle's reprieve on its front page, with the headline, 'Dramatic Scene in the Death Cell'. The paper carried a photograph of the telegram that had been sent by the Scottish Home Department in Edinburgh to Lord Provost Stephen at Aberdeen Town House. It read, 'Case of Robert James Boyle now lying under sentence of death. The Secretary of State has decided to advise that execution of capital sentence shall be commuted to imprisonment for life.' Within minutes of receiving the telegram at 11.45 a.m., Lord Provost George Stephen, wearing his ceremonial robes and gold chain of office, and the town clerk, Mr J C Rennie, were driven to the jail. There, they were met by the prison governor, Major M P Lothian, and taken to Boyle's cell, where Aberdeen's number one citizen broke the good news.

Afterwards, the Lord Provost told the newspaper, 'Boyle was lying in bed, when we saw him, but he didn't look ill. We understood he had a chill. I merely made the formal announcement that he had been reprieved and Boyle thanked me. There was no other discussion – talk was not encouraged.' He added, 'I don't believe in hanging and because of that I was happy to be the bearer of the good tidings.'

In Paisley, Boyle's parents had organised a reprieve petition and were awaiting the delivery of forms from a printer. Boyle's father returned to the slaters' yard where he worked to be told by his boss, 'Your son has been reprieved.' He was then told to go home. But, after sending messages to his wife and his son's spouse, the relieved man went off to repair a garden wall to keep his mind occupied.

LEGAL PRECEDENTS

Apart from the Boyle baby-killer case, there have been only three other modern-day Scottish murder cases where there has been a conviction without a body. In 1962, Francis John Kilbride (32) threw a child into the River Kelvin in Glasgow. He was found guilty of murder but, at the time of his trial in April that year, the body of the four-year-old girl had not been found. However, a month after he was sentenced to life imprisonment, the missing body was discovered.

In November 1989, a Bristol drugs courier was shot after unwittingly digging his own grave on Fenwick Moor in Ayrshire. His body has never been found but three men were convicted of murder and of the theft of his consignment of drugs, after one of them gave evidence against his fellow accused.

The disappearance of mother-of-two Mrs Arlene Fraser, from her Elgin home in April 1998, sparked a massive police investigation, which finally ended on 29 January 2003, when her husband, Nat, was given life for her murder. After the three-week High Court trial in Edinburgh, Lord Mackay of Drumadoon told Nat Fraser that he must serve at least twenty-five years. Grampian detectives later revealed how a forensic lip-reader deciphered a conversation Fraser had had with a visitor while he was in Porterfield Prison, Inverness. The meeting was caught on security cameras and left detectives in no doubt that Fraser had killed his wife and dismembered her body, no trace of which has ever been found.

The Boyle murder mirrors a child-killing of bygone times. In

1749, Anne Philp, the wife of an exciseman, was found guilty of murdering her year-old child by drowning it in the sea off Stonehaven. She was seen walking towards the sea with her child and then retracing her footsteps soon after, carrying only its clothes. Its body was never recovered and her counsel argued that the murder was not proven, as the child had been given to the accused's friends. Philp was found guilty but, two weeks before she was due to be executed, she received a free pardon.

9

TRAIL OF HORROR

1966

What was the dark secret of 27 Logie Avenue? Neighbours presumed that the family living in the ground-floor flat of a Middlefield tenement had gone away. For there was no sign of steel erector Adam Sherriffs (38), his wife, Isabella (42) and the two youngsters. They were Mrs Sherriffs' younger son by a previous marriage, Murray McCabe (13), a pupil of Powis School, and the couple's three-year-old daughter, Jacqueline. Mr Sherriffs, a powerfully built man with dark hair, worked for a city construction firm and was, at the time, employed at the Balnagask housing scheme in Torry. The couple had met eight years earlier, in 1958, and were married at Aberdeen Registrar's Office in May 1960.

When Bella Sherriffs' elder son, John McCabe (21), a crewman on the Aberdeen trawler *Summervale*, returned from a trip, he went to stay at the flat. Since their marriage a year earlier, he and his teenage wife, Eileen, had not found a home and, on occasions, the couple had been forced to live apart, staying with relatives. When John got into the flat, it looked as if nobody had been living there for days. The bedroom, where his mother and stepfather slept, was locked and he didn't have the key. Next day Eileen, who had been living with her mother in Torry, joined her husband at the flat.

John later told a *Scottish Daily Express* reporter, 'There was no sign of any violence but I wondered where they all were.' The stocky, broad-shouldered deck-hand visited his grandmother, Mrs Georgina Gray, in Causewayend. His grandmother told John that, while he had been at sea, his stepfather had called on her and told her that Bella had walked out on him. Mr Sherriffs, who was accompanied by Jacqueline, had phoned John's company to find out when his boat was due in. From what he gathered from his grandmother, John believed that his brother, Murray, and his stepsister, Jacqueline, were staying with Mr Sherriffs' father at Blackdog, a hamlet a few miles north of the city.

But the truth was far more sinister. On the afternoon of Wednesday 27 July 1966, there was a fateful knock on the door at No. 27 and the police broke the news that Mr Sherriffs had been found dead. Earlier that day, retired farmer Hector Strachan was walking the north bank of the River Don when he stumbled across the blood-chilling sight of a hanged man. Sherriffs had hanged himself from a tree in the grounds of Balgownie Eventide Home at the Bridge of Don, about three miles from his home. In his pocket was a note that outlined the tragic fate of his wife and the two youngsters. He had murdered them.

Violent death had come to No. 27 when Sherriffs strangled Bella and Murray and then hid the bodies under the floorboards. Police found them below a hatch in the hallway behind the front door. Then, hand-in-hand with auburn-haired Jacqueline, he made his way to Balgownie. In a cornfield, next to grounds of the eventide home, he strangled the little girl he idolised. He then walked 150 yards to a small wood overlooking the Don and took his own life. After the trail of horror led police to 27 Logie Avenue, the flat became the scene of intense activity as murder-team detectives moved in. They were joined by the procurator fiscal and a police doctor. A policeman stood guard at the front door and only tenants in the three-storey tenement were allowed past. A corporation joiner was called and, over two hours after detectives arrived at the death flat, two coffins were removed to the police mortuary. John and Eileen McCabe had gone to an upstairs neighbour when police first arrived to search the flat. As Eileen left for her mother's home, she glanced into the death flat. The hatch behind the front door had been raised. 'It was horrible to think we had been staying there without knowing,' she told a man from the *Scottish Daily Express*.

Later that night, a joint statement was issued by Aberdeen CID chief, Detective Superintendent Harry Halcrow, and his Aberdeen-shire Constabulary counterpart, Bill Glennie. The county force was involved because, in those days, they had jurisdiction over the area where the bodies of Sherriffs and his daughter had been found. At their press conference at Aberdeen City Police head-quarters, Mr Halcrow confirmed the grim discoveries and said inquiries were continuing. But, privately, the police knew the case was closed. Next day, the 28th, the city's procurator-fiscal, Mr Andrew McNicol, said, 'Police inquiries indicate that no other person is involved in this tragedy. It is not proposed to issue any further statements.' After police had stopped probing, the city was still asking, 'Why?'

Dark-haired Mrs Sherriffs, a hard-working housewife, had taken on jobs in cafes as well as caring for her family. At Balnagask, her husband's workmate said, 'Adam was a very quiet, steady-going chap and he was a good worker. I don't know what happened to cause this.' Even the neighbours in Logie Avenue were baffled. 'The folk around here just don't understand it,' said one tearful woman. In an interview to the *Scottish Daily Express*, John McCabe said the couple had enjoyed a happy marriage. 'My stepfather adored my mother and wanted to be with her all the time. He loved Murray and adored Jacqueline,' he added. John indicated to *Daily Record* reporter, Jim Gillespie, that there had been tension in the family and it was no secret his stepfather drank. John added, 'But I never dreamed that anything like this would happen.' He also told the *Express*, 'This has been a nightmare. I wish someone could tell me it is not true.'

The Saltoun Arms pub today. Its ornate doorway existed when butcher James Harrow fatally stabbed two workmates in 1901.

The latest photo of the prisoner Harrow.

HARROW'S HABITS AND CHARACTER.

Yesterday in the vicinity of the tragedy and among those who know Harrow, the murder was the sole subject of conversation. In the light of the gruesome circumstances, many little matters which otherwise would have been forgotten regarding the habits of the accused

This newspaper illustration of killer James Harrow was based on an official police photograph taken at Lodge Walk shortly before his appearance before Sheriff Burnet.

Senior detectives examine the spot where June Cruickshank was found dying on a January evening in 1961. Detective Chief Inspector Donald McIntosh (left) headed the murder probe. He is accompanied by Detective Inspector Hamish Johnston.

On her way home from a local shop in Great Northern Road, six-year-old June Cruickshank was lured into this cul-de-sac by her killer.

The Lair. Police and CID men prepare to exhume the body of seven-year-old George Forbes from the floor of this Commerce Street greenhouse on 16 November 1963.

The vital clue of a one-shilling piece, kept secret by Aberdeen CID, helped trap double child-killer James Oliphant.

Urquhart Road child-murderer Jeannie Donald in happier times. She was sentenced to death for killing Helen Priestly in 1934, but was reprieved.

Daily Record

I LOVE MY HUSBAND'S KILLER . . .

YES TO

MURDER widow Margaret Guyan talked last night of her love for her husband's killer.

"My heart is with Harry Burnett," she told the 'Record.' "I'm sorry for what has happened—but I love Harry."

As she spoke, her lover, 21-year-old Henry John Burnett was in his cell at Craiginches Prison, Aberdeen, sentenced to death

I have to believe

Hours earlier, in the High Court at Aberdeen, Burnett had been found guilty, by a maority verdict, of the murder of seaman Thomas Guyan.

Last night in her home at 14 Jackson Terrace, Aberdeen—the house where she saw her husband killed—Mrs. Guyan, 25-year-old mother of two, said:

"*No matter what anyone else says, I have to believe in Henry Burnett. I can't really say why, but I know I still love him.*

"Tommy was a good husband—but not a good father.

"Tommy was at sea when I met Harry Burnett. We fell in love."

During the trial, in

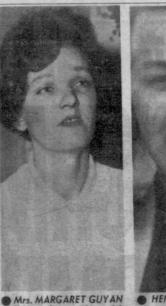
● Mrs. MARGARET GUYAN "My heart is with Harry."

● HENRY BURNETT . . . . . . sentenced to death yesterday.

Scotpix

Henry Burnett, the last man to hang in Scotland, was hot news. He proposed to his lover Margaret Guyan after killing her husband.

A lone policeman stands guard at 14 Jackson Terrace after the 1963 shotgun murder.

Author Norman Adams (second left of the tree, facing camera) reported on the scene outside Craiginches Prison on the day of Henry Burnett's execution.

Prison chaplain Rev. John Dickson leaves Craiginches after the hanging. His silver cross was the last thing Burnett saw on the scaffold.

Marshall H. Glover, Aberdeen

Police and fishers search for the body of Betty Hadden after her severed forearm was found on the Torry foreshore of Aberdeen's navigation channel in December 1945.

The Second World War had ended four months earlier, but it was the Betty Hadden murder mystery that grabbed the headlines.

Evening Express/Aberdeen Central Library

Evening Express FINAL

Sunshine Bleach — LIGHTENS BRIGHTENS WHITENS

Haig

No. 21,117 (Estab. 1879). 1½d.   THURSDAY, DECEMBER 13, 1945.   A KEMSLEY NEWSPAPER.

Police Hunt For Clues In Forearm Mystery

The Missing Girl

Intensive Search Of Aberdeen Beach For Traces Of Missing Girl

WHAT HAS BEFALLEN BETTY HADDEN, THE MISSING 18-YEAR-OLD ABERDEEN GIRL, WHOSE SAWN-OFF FOREARM WAS FOUND YESTERDAY ON THE FORESHORE OF ABERDEEN NAVIGATION CHANNEL?
THE GRIM POSSIBILITY THAT SHE HAS BEEN DONE TO DEATH CONFRONTS THE POLICE.

With only the girl's dismembered forearm and hand, and the knowledge that she was last seen walking along Castle Street late on Monday night, to work on, Aberdeen C.I.D. officers continued to-day their investigations into the baffling mystery.

The search of the beach and the rocky coast at Aberdeen and in the neighbourhood, which was halted by the fall of

POLICE APPEAL TO COMPANIONS

Aberdeen City Police are anxious to interview the four girls who were seen in Betty Hadden's company, opposite the Town House, late on Monday night.

36 Dachau Accused To Die

Glasgow Murders
100 "Ginger" Hair Men Questioned

Glasgow police have checked up on about 100 persons with "ginger" hair who otherwise answered the description of the wanted man in connection with the Pollokshields East stabbing double murder.

In every case those questioned have been able to satisfy the detectives that they had nothing to do with the affair.

The woman victim, Ann Withers (36), died almost immediately after being shot. The second victim of the armed bandit's attack, Robert Gough (15), porter, died in the infirmary last night.

Before his death the boy was able to give a minute description of the assailant.

Scottish Daily Express/The Mitchell Library

Scotpix

Alexander Stewart, known as the 'Phantom', killed twice and was sent to Carstairs to join his brother, Frank.

A police photographer captures the grim aftermath of Mrs Shirley Stewart's murder at Moir Crescent in 1970. She fled from the butcher's shop at No. 29 but collapsed moments later outside the grocer's shop next door.

Aberdeen Journals Ltd

James Connor Smith puffs on a cigarette to steady his nerves after being jailed for life for a fatal stabbing in a city pub in October 1964.

At the height of the Dr Brenda Page murder inquiry, Sergeant Ian Burnett puts up a police poster in a corner-shop window – just 50 yards from the scientist's home in Allan Street.

Cab-driver George Murdoch's taxi stands abandoned in Pitfodels Station Road on the night of his murder in September 1983. His killer has never been traced.

The pool room of the Covenanter Bar in Kincorth, where Graham Duncan committed a brutal murder four days before Christmas 1985. Note the festive decorations.

10

MURDER IN A GARDEN SUBURB

1987

On a murky July evening, Julie King, a bright, happy two-year-old, was brutally battered to death with a stone in the Aberdeen garden suburb of Westhill. The dying girl was found in undergrowth at the entrance to Crombie Primary School after she had disappeared from outside her nearby home where she had been playing. The alarm was raised by four teenagers, one of whom turned out to be her killer.

The crime horrified the suburb's 8,000 residents. Detectives, led by CID boss, Chief Superintendent Jim McLeod, set up an incident room at the school, less than 200 yards from the child's quiet cul-de-sac home. Door-to-door calls were carried out. A special hot-line enabled the public to phone in with any relevant information. One theory was that Julie had been snatched from outside her home and police advised parents to accompany young children when they went out.

Three days after the murder, a fifteen-year-old schoolboy was detained by Grampian Police. He later made a brief appearance at Aberdeen Sheriff Court charged with Julie's murder. Golden-haired Julie was the only child of oil worker Brian King (27) and his wife, Irene (25). At the time, the couple were expecting their second child. On 22 September 1987, the schoolboy appeared at the High Court in Aberdeen accused of murdering Julie. It was alleged that he had forced her to the ground, held her by the neck, compressed her chest and abdomen and struck her repeatedly on the head with a stone. He denied the charge.

Before the start of the trial, the judge, Lord Dunpark, directed that the accused should not be named by the media because of his age. Section 169 of the Criminal Procedure (Scotland) Act states that no report of any case should disclose the name, address, school or any other particulars which might lead to the identification of any person under the age of sixteen concerned in the proceedings.

Mr King told the jury of eight women and seven men that, on Wednesday 15 July, he had taken Julie out to the garage to show her a desk and chair he was painting for her. After tea, they both went outside. Her father resumed painting while Julie played at the garage door. She decided she wanted to play on her bike and he changed her shoes for a pair of 'Roland Rat' Wellington boots. He checked on his daughter periodically as she was playing or watching a neighbour repair his car.

Before Julie went missing, at about 6.40 p.m., she had asked if she could have an ice cream when a van arrived outside her house. She hadn't eaten her tea so her dad said she couldn't have one. Mr King started searching for Julie with a neighbour and, after phoning the police, he came across her lying in a clump of bushes at the entrance to the primary school. Some other people, including a nurse who was tending to Julie, were already there. 'I thought she was still alive,' said Mr King. He heard a groan but couldn't feel any pulse. The child was taken by ambulance to hospital in Aberdeen where she subsequently died.

Ice-cream van driver, Colin Forbes (40), of Heatheryfold Circle, Aberdeen, saw Julie outside her home saying loudly that she wanted an ice-cream. He was leaving the street when the accused asked to buy some loose cigarettes. On the following evening, he saw the accused again in the same area and had joked, 'You're the number one suspect.' The boy laughed and said something about being in the clear. In cross-examination, Mr Forbes told Mr Donald Macaulay QC, defending, that the remark was said as a joke. He had no idea whether the boy had been interviewed by the police.

A fifteen-year-old youth told how the accused had joined him and two other boys on the fateful evening and said he had found a little girl with blood pouring out of her head. They had not believed him at first. But, when they went to the bushes, the witness saw what he took to be a doll in pink clothes. On closer inspection, he saw it was a little girl lying there. She had blood and mud on the right-hand side of her face and she gave a faint moan. Before the ambulance arrived, the accused said he thought the girl might have been struck on the head with a stone. He later asked the other youths, 'What if she wakes up in hospital and starts pointing at one of us and saying, "It's him, it's him!"?'

At 7.15 p.m., the youths rang the doorbell of qualified nurse Claire Christie (30) who, on being told about the injured girl, went to see if she could help. Before returning to her house to call the ambulance and police, she wrapped the child in a towel and placed her on her side. By an ironic twist, the nurse asked the accused to make sure she remained in that position. The youth looked after the injured girl until the ambulance arrived. On the second day of the trial, the court was cleared after a young juryman collapsed while listening to the medical evidence given by a female doctor. She ran from the witness box and tended the man on the floor. After an adjournment, the judge excused the juror further duty and the trial continued with fourteen jurors.

Evidence from the police added to a day of drama. Detective Inspector Alexander Den, (44), arrested the youth at his home after he found a number of discrepancies in his statements. He said the accused's status had changed from that of witness to suspect. The youth's father accompanied his son to police headquarters in Aberdeen. When Inspector Den told the boy he was suspected of being involved, he became very distressed and cried most of the time. His father was also upset. At one point during the interview, the father interjected, telling his son he would always be his pal and asked him to tell the truth. The youth told the police that Julie had been following him about and he had tried to frighten her so that she would leave. She had sat beside him on a fence at Crombie School. She had fallen against a wall and had struck her head. Inspector Den and his colleague, Detective-Constable Ian McGrory, left the room and, on their return, told the accused they believed the little girl had been hit on the head a number of times. The youth then admitted that Julie wouldn't stop screaming so he had dropped a stone on her head once and then he had left her lying there.

On another occasion, the two detectives left the room, having indicated the accused would be charged in the presence of a solicitor, Detective Constable John Morgan took note of a conversation between the distraught father and son. The father took the youth's head in his hands and said, 'I'm clutching at straws. Did you only say it to get them [the detectives] off your back?' His son replied that he hadn't. 'Did you smack the girlie?' asked his father. The youth said, 'Aye, I did.'

On the third and final day, the accused went into the box where he was warned by his counsel, Mr Macaulay, that this was his last opportunity to tell the truth. The youth said Julie had followed him from her street after he had bought cigarettes from the ice-cream van. She followed as he made his way to the school playground where he usually went for a smoke. She asked if he liked her 'Roland Rat' boots. He was embarrassed and tried to get her to leave. She went off to get her bike and he hid. When she returned, he jumped from behind a wall at the school and shouted 'Boo!' at her. She fell back and struck her head on the wall. She kept screaming and he picked up a stone and hit her. He threw the stone at her from about two feet. He then ran away but returned soon afterwards to find that the girl was not where he had left her. He thought Julie had gone home. But he heard a moan and went into the bushes. He then saw how bad it was.

It took the jury an hour and a half to find the schoolboy guilty by a majority of Julie's murder. Lord Dunpark ordered him to be detained without limit of time. The accused showed no emotion at the verdict. His mother stifled a sob with a hand while her equally distraught husband lowered his head. Julie's parents were also in court to hear the sentence. Outside the court Julie's father said they were relieved the trial was all over. 'Now we will just get back to normal – or as normal as we can,' he told reporters.

Twelve days before the trial had begun, Mrs King had given birth to a lusty boy. Smiling for the first time, Mr King, a keen amateur footballer, said his son would make a good goal scorer and could play one day for Celtic.

Bushes no longer grow at the entrance of Crombie School. They invoked too many painful memories for residents and parents taking their children to classes and so they were uprooted by Grampian Regional Council.

11

BIRTHDAY TAUNT

1955

On the bleakest of winter Saturdays, William Henry McKerron made his way through Aberdeen's snowy streets to confront his wayward wife, Alice. Married life had been nineteen months of walk-outs and bitter rows, despite efforts by the merchant-navy man to make it work. It was before nine in the morning of 19 February 1955 when McKerron reached her address in Woodside.

The country was in the grip of terrible weather. Convoys of snowploughs were out in force in the north-east. Grantown-on-Spey had endured 52 degrees of frost, while grave-diggers were forced to use pick-axes. Seven thousand Rangers fans were struggling through drifts for an important Scottish Cup tie at Pittodrie.

As McKerron entered the tenement at 11 Ferrier Crescent, children shouted excitedly as they sledged in the street. Shortly afterwards, housewife Mary Main met McKerron on the stairway. He told her, 'Fetch the police. There's been trouble.' McKerron had killed his wife. It was the day of his twenty-third birthday.

Two days later McKerron, a tall, slim figure wearing a suit and blue open-necked shirt, appeared at Aberdeen Sheriff Court in connection with his wife's death. Sheriff Sam McDonald remanded him in custody for further examination. Under the original indictment, McKerron was accused of murdering his wife by throttling her. But, when he appeared in the dock at the High Court in Aberdeen on Tuesday 31 May, the advocate-depute, Mr Douglas Reith, accepted a plea of culpable homicide.

McKerron had married Alice Burnett, who was two years younger than him, in July 1953. But, said Mr Reith, she appeared to have been of loose moral character and had apparently consorted with various men, mainly seamen. Their marriage was blighted with quarrels. McKerron had attempted to get her to settle down but without much success. Latterly, they lived apart – although they met from time to time, mainly in pubs. By then, McKerron was drinking fairly heavily.

On the night before the killing, the estranged couple met in a pub. A quarrel developed in the course of the evening and, next day, McKerron called at the first-floor flat in Ferrier Crescent where his wife had sub-let a room from her stepfather, Frederick Burnett. A female friend was also visiting Alice and McKerron said he wanted to speak to his wife alone. Reluctantly, Alice went with him into the bedroom. Minutes later, McKerron left the room, locking it behind him. He said words to the effect that he had strangled his wife. He unlocked the door when police arrived and admitted what he had done. Mr Reith said there seemed to be a possibility of a degree of diminished responsibility at the time of the offence. McKerron's counsel, Mr Ewan Stewart, said the accused's culpability was of a lesser degree than might first appear and the consequences of his act were quite unforeseen by him.

Aberdeen-born McKerron came from a broken home, his parents having divorced when he was thirteen. He proved an excellent pupil at primary school – quiet, attentive and patient. His teacher, said Mr Stewart, thought he had the 'makings of a very good man'. He was the dux of his class and won a bursary to Robert Gordon's College in Aberdeen. His career in the merchant navy began in 1948. After training school, he went to sea where his ability and general conduct were of the highest standard.

Mr Stewart then told of McKerron's unhappy marriage and its tragic ending. Although McKerron knew the sort of woman he was marrying, his attachment to her was so strong that this did not deter him. He hoped his wife would settle down to a normal home life. In the beginning, things seemed to be working out but Mrs McKerron did not make a home for her husband. While he was at sea, he paid a generous financial allowance for his wife. The money was paid through his father but the allowance was cut off when Mrs McKerron's conduct began to deteriorate again.

In October 1954, it was apparent that she had resumed her life on the streets. Statements from her female associates showed she knew that her husband cared deeply for her but she was unable to interest herself in family life and to shake off her sordid way of life. After nineteen months of marriage, Mrs McKerron had reached a very low level of degradation. She drank heavily and associated with men – mostly foreign sailors. McKerron still hoped to rehabilitate his wife and save their marriage, said Mr Stewart, but, on the eve of the tragedy, he found her talking to sailors in a dockland pub. He asked her to leave but the subsequent quarrel spilled into the street and the police had to move them on. Mrs McKerron had left the scene alone.

Next morning, McKerron had gone to Ferrier Crescent to tackle his wife about the previous night. She was in the scullery with another woman and that woman's children. He told her he wanted to speak to her alone. Mr Stewart said that what took place in the bedroom was only the accused's version of what had happened next. McKerron had asked for an explanation but his wife said she was too drunk to remember. She remarked that his premature arrival at the pub had spoiled her chance of a pick-up. Her brazen taunt had made McKerron so angry that he had grabbed her by the throat to frighten her, added Mr Stewart. She had taken a step backwards and tripped over a chair. When he realised she was dead, a shocked McKerron immediately sent for the police.

Mr Stewart told the judge, Lord Carmont:

Here is a young man of good character who finds himself in his present position through being goaded beyond reasonable endurance by a woman for whom he had tried to do everything and against whom, in the end, he raised his hands in anger with consequences totally unexpected and unforeseen by him.

Lord Carmont told McKerron that he had borne in mind the moral conduct of the deceased woman and the provocation he must have had. 'But,' he added, 'you have taken into your own hands the administration of what you regarded as punishment.' There were gasps from the public gallery when the judge passed a sentence of twelve years' imprisonment, but McKerron, left the dock without a show of emotion.

Beyond the courtroom walls, the country was suffering from a crippling strikes. At Balmoral, on the day that McKerron was sentenced, the Queen, in the presence of her Privy Council, signed a proclamation declaring a state of emergency to deal with the national dock strike. McKerron had remained silent in court but, it will be remembered, on the day he was arrested, a big cup tie was scheduled for that afternoon at Pittodrie. As McKerron eyed the vanguard of fans heading for the match (44,647 would eventually squeeze into the ground), he dryly told the arresting detectives in the police car taking him to Lodge Walk, 'You'll not be seeing your football today.'

Three years later, Serious Crime Squad detectives would return again to Ferrier Crescent.

12

AN INSPECTOR CALLS

1958

It had been a hectic and fun-packed weekend in Aberdeen. An estimated 25,000 Glasgow Fair holiday-makers had arrived by road, rail and courtesy of British European Airways, to take advantage of the warm and pleasant weather and flock to the beach and parks. There was a mass pipe-band display at the Duthie Park and impromptu pop sing-songs at the beach. All the city dance halls were crowded on the Saturday night. But not everyone had caught the holiday mood. The directors of the Pleasure Beach were furious. Their outdoor fun-fair was closed because the council wouldn't grant them a Sunday licence. But council-run putting and bowling greens and tennis courts were open.

On Monday 21 July 1958, Harry Webber, the Pleasure Beach's director of publicity, was angry at a newspaper's claim that Aberdeen was becoming a haven for pickpockets. A CID spokesman also scotched the slur. Far from the madding crowds that evening, John Brandie was listening to a BBC radio play in the sitting room of his ground-floor flat when there was an urgent knock on the window. His choice of play is not known. He could have tuned into *A Quiet Corner* or *Inspector Scott Investigates*. Either way, it would have been a relevant but ironic choice, as it turned out. For the trawlerman's relaxation was about to be rudely shattered and, before the day was done, a police inspector would call at the three-floored tenement at 21 Ferrier Crescent.

The man at the window was Eric Pirie Smith Stephen, a labourer and former school chum of Brandie, who lived with his wife and family in the flat above. When Brandie went to the door, he found Stephen waiting for him. He asked Brandie if he would go upstairs with him and, then, while they were still on the landing, Stephen said, 'Will you go for the police, Jackie? I have just choked Isabel.'

Stephen (26) appeared quite normal but his demeanour crumbled when he entered his flat. His young wife, Isabella, a mother of three children, aged, five, four and nearly two, was dead in bed. There was something tied round her neck. Medical evidence would show that Mrs Stephen had died from asphyxia caused by strangulation. First, manual pressure had been applied by thumbs on the front of her neck and then a white blouse was used as a ligature. The bedclothes were up to her chest and the youngest child was asleep by the side of her dead mother. Brandie left his friend shocked and distressed in an armchair while he hurried to phone the police. Stephen was still sitting in the chair when he came back. The sleeping child, whose second birthday would fall on the very day her mother was buried, was now restless and swung a foot across the body. Brandie gently picked up the wee girl, carried her to the other bedroom and put her to bed with her two older brothers. Brandie sat on the arm of the chair beside Stephen who told him, 'I seen it coming, Jackie.'

When Detective Inspector Harry Halcrow called at the flat, he found Stephen sitting dejectedly in the armchair. The inspector cautioned him in the scullery and Stephen confessed, 'I lost the heid.' There was no apparent sign of a struggle between Stephen and his wife. At the central police office, when charged with murder, Stephen said he would wait to see what his solicitor advised.

Next day, the *Evening Express* noted, 'In the flat where Mrs Stephen was found, a lone policeman and the family budgie today kept a silent watch.' There was a faint echo here of another time and another murder. In 1857, journalist William Carnie, nosing around the house where John Booth, the last man to be publicly hanged in Aberdeen, stabbed his wife's mother, left us a poignant description of a little caged bird singing above the corpse, 'as blithely as if it had been its native bush'.

Brandie went to the police mortuary to identify Mrs Stephen's body, while his wife, Gladys, stayed at home to look after her their own children and talk to reporters. The Stephens had only been staying at No. 21 for a short time. They had befriended the Brandies and had often had tea in their home. The couple had appeared there at lunchtime on the Monday and Mrs Brandie last saw the victim that evening when Mrs Stephen called on her to repay a debt. Mrs Brandie spoke well of Mrs Stephen, a plumpish woman, cheerful and helpful, who, she said, lived for her youngsters. The dead woman had been married for more than six years and had celebrated her twenty-fourth birthday five days earlier. Her children were too young to know the awful truth and were given refuge in their maternal grandmother's home in Froghall.

Mrs Isabella McKenzie (51) had last seen her daughter when she left No. 21. at 6.10 p.m. on the Tuesday. She said Isabel was in fine spirits and had promised to call on her the following day. Mrs McKenzie had arranged to return to her daughter's later in the evening but she had been occupied at her work as a cleaner at the Trades College. 'Now I wish I had gone round,' she told the *Evening Express*. 'It's a horrible business.' She would not be drawn on what they had discussed. Their conversation would remain confidential until Stephen's High Court trial in the autumn. However, the press hinted that the couple had lived apart on several occasions.

Shortly after his arrest, the slimly built Stephen, dressed in light blue jeans and an open-necked shirt, appeared briefly at Aberdeen Sheriff Court in connection with his wife's death. After the usual formalities, he was remanded in custody for further inquiries. Stephen was less casually dressed when he made a brief appearance in the same dock at a High Court Pleading Diet. Dressed in a brown suit, blue zip-up jersey, white shirt and a tie, he stood with his hands clasped behind his back as the charge was read out. It alleged that, on 21 July 1958, in the house occupied by his wife,

Isabella Campbell Clayton McKenzie or Stephen, at 21 Ferrier Crescent, Aberdeen, he assaulted her, compressed her throat with his hands, tied a blouse round her throat and murdered her. His agent, Mr W H Rutherford, said Stephen pleaded not guilty and Sheriff Archibald Hamilton remitted him to the High Court in Aberdeen on 14 October.

The High Court heard that the couple's short married life had had more than its share of rows and reconciliation since they had married on 22 November 1951. Mrs Stephen was then seventeen. John Brandie, who held a hushed High Court in the palm of his hand as he described finding Mrs Stephen's dead body, also revealed that the accused had returned to the family home only a week to ten days before the tragedy. He told Mr Douglas Reith QC, defending, that they seemed to be on good terms but Mrs Stephen had said he was back for 'a sort of week's trial'. Mr Reith asked, 'Did she say anything about how this trial was going?' and Brandie replied, 'No. Everything seemed to be okay.' The deceased's mother, Mrs McKenzie, then disclosed her conversation with her daughter at their final meeting. 'Mother,' Mrs Stephen had said, 'I've taken him back but I think I have made a mistake. But there are two days left and I might put him out.' Mrs McKenzie claimed she did not understand the significance of the two days mentioned by her daughter.

Her two sons, Robert and William McKenzie, described quarrels between the couple and their separation after Stephen had slashed his own wrists with a razor blade while living with their mother. Court proceedings were dramatically halted when Robert denied that he had asked his brother-in-law to quit the house. Stephen leapt to his feet in the dock and stabbed an accusing finger at him. 'You're a liar,' he shouted. 'You've been lying all the time.' Shocked officials watched as Stephen was forcibly restrained by his police escort. A few minutes later, Robert McKenzie staggered against the handrail of the witness box and collapsed. He was treated by a police doctor but was unable to resume his evidence.

William Stephen (61), the accused's father, limped into the box on crutches and was allowed to give his evidence seated. He admitted trying to stop his son marrying Isabella because he thought they were too young. He understood that the girl's mother had thought the same. In July 1952, his son had returned alone to live with his parents at 2 Ferrier Gardens. His son had also lived at that address on his return from Kingseat Hospital, where he had been a voluntary patient after his suicide bid. The accused had gone back to live with his wife the day after one of his children had called at 2 Ferrier Gardens to ask his father to go for a walk.

On the evening of 21 July, Mr Stephen recalled how his son had visited him for only a few minutes. He had looked in on his mother who was asleep. Asked why he hadn't come across earlier to watch the Commonwealth Games boxing on TV, he had shrugged his shoulders and said he wasn't bothered. He then walked out. Mr Stephen described his son as a 'very fine fellow' when he stayed with his parents. They never rowed.

In evidence, Eric Stephen said that, despite the quarrels and marriage break-up, he was fond of his wife and three children. Even during their separation, he was allowed to visit his wife and family. They were quite friendly towards each other. Stephen had worked for a spell in Doncaster until his return to Aberdeen, on 7 July 1958, when his wife agreed to a reconciliation. He believed he was back with her for good.

But, on the evening of 21 July, his wife delivered a bombshell. He said she had ordered him out of the house. He told the court, 'She said the kids were not wanting me there.' He could remember nothing of what happened next until leaving the house to go downtown to give himself up. He changed his mind and returned to the death flat. He then went downstairs to ask John Brandie to fetch the police. He told his defence counsel he had never attacked his wife in the past and he certainly had no intention of harming her on the fateful night.

The court was told that his failure to hold a job and to handle his financial affairs were at the root of his marital problems. For the Crown, Mr G C Carmichael suggested that the accused had strangled his wife in a fit of temper. Stephen shook his head and whispered, 'My memory is very vague but I remember the argument. The next thing I realised was that she was dead."

Two medical witnesses, called by the defence, were Dr Andrew Wyllie, physician superintendent of Cornhill Hospital, Aberdeen, and Dr Ronald Stewart, his counterpart at Kingseat Hospi-tal, Aberdeenshire. Dr Wyllie said the accused was neither insane nor intellectually defective but was immature and suffered from a disorder of feelings, temper and habits which made him only partially responsible for his actions. Dr Stewart said that Stephen's attack on his wife was impulsive and unpremeditated. Coupled with his attempted suicide, this showed that, under certain conditions of stress, his self-control was diminished to the extent that, momentarily, he might be said to have shown diminished responsibility for his actions.

In his address to the jury, Mr Reith, defending, asked the jury to bring a verdict not of murder but of culpable homicide. He said it was a case of diminished responsibility. He told them, 'I am not suggesting that Stephen is insane but what I am maintaining is that, at the time he laid hands on his wife, he was in such a situation of stress that he was not fully responsible for his actions.' But, in his direction to the jury, Lord Wheatley made it abundantly clear that the law of the country must not be subordinated to medical theories. The jury of seven men and eight women took only twenty-three minutes to find Stephen guilty of murder by a majority. He listened calmly as Lord Wheatley told him, 'You have been found guilty of murder, not capital murder, and for that offence the law prescribes but one sentence, which I am duty bound to impose. I accordingly sentence you to imprisonment for life.'

Stephen's moment of madness had left three youngsters mother-less. After the verdict, a tearful Mrs McKenzie, the deceased's mother, said that she was glad, for the children's sake, that the case was over. They had tried to get Isabella not to marry Stephen but her daughter was so much in love she could not see his faults. Mrs McKenzie visited her grandchildren in an Aberdeen Corporation home once a week. It was her wish that they would, one day, get a proper home of their own and that they would be able to make a fresh start in life.

Exactly one month after Stephen had strangled his wife, a second murder of a spouse occurred when, in another part of Aberdeen, a man brutally killed his wife. The paths of these two wife-murderers would cross more than once. After Stephen had appeared at his High Court Pleading Diet on 3 October, the next to be up in the dock was William Whyte, a middle-aged man with dark, grey-streaked hair. These two accused men would appear again in the same courthouse to be dealt with by the same High Court judge.

13

SHOTS IN THE NIGHT

1958

Rosehill Farmhouse no longer stood alone on a distant hillside overlooking Aberdeen. It had long since ceased to be a working farm and its days were numbered. Even though news reporters would describe it as being on the outskirts of the city, it was actually located at the summit of Cairncry Road. Ranks of post-war prefabs encroached on its rough, time-worn stone walls and soon its name would survive only on new street maps along with other vanished local farms such as Upper Mastrick, Oldtown, Northfield and Granitehill.

When I first saw it on a miserable, wet morning in August 1958, Rosehill, a traditional two-storey farmhouse with slated roof and dormer windows, had white rambling roses at the front door and garden gate. It had been incorporated into the prefab colony and was also known to the postman as 12 Blackthorn Crescent. A past generation would, no doubt, have spent evenings in the old farmhouse singing bothy ballads, telling ghost stories or mending socks by the flicker of an oil lamp.

On the dreich night of Monday 18 August 1958, some of the residents of the prefabs had had their eyes glued to their television screens. For these stay-at-homes, it was a welcome relief from the atrocious weekend weather which had seen Banchory experience its worst cloudburst and flooding in living memory. On the 'box' that evening, the top offerings from the BBC (In those days, there was only one channel – no Grampian or even BBC2.) included *The Phil Silvers Show*, *Henry Hall's Guest Night*, a movie magazine show called *Picture Parade* and an appearance by singer Michael Holliday. These programmes were followed by the news, with the close-down at eleven.

Rosehill Farmhouse was occupied by the Whytes. The head of the family was dealer William Whyte (50). His wife, Elizabeth (43), was a mother of ten children. There were nine boys, whose ages ranged from twenty-four to eight, and one girl, who, at six, was the youngest of this large brood. That August night, most of the family were in bed. A nineteen-year-old son was away serving with the army.

Orchestra leader Henry Hall would have been half-way through his show when next-door neighbour Ron Grant, at No. 14, heard the sound of breaking glass. Mr Grant (21), an apprentice brick-layer, told newspaper reporters, 'That's what started it. It was a big smash. It must have been a window falling in.' Grant nipped round to the front of the old farmhouse. He heard a young man's voice ring out, saying, 'Haud her head up, she's pouring bleed!' Grant's startled gaze then followed the figure of a running man being chased along the street. The dying woman was taken by van by her two eldest sons to hospital where she died soon after admission.

The Milnes, who lived in the former steading at the farm, added to the apparent mystery. As the couple sat at their fireside with their son Willie, they heard 'an awful rumble just like thunder'. When their son eventually ventured out, the close was teeming with police and an ambulance had just arrived. Most of the other neighbours were watching TV and could add little. 'We just heard breaking glass and didn't see anything until it was all by,' said a Mrs Ross. Mrs Agnes MacDonald, at No. 20, heard a bang but there was no one at her door. Only when her daughter arrived home did she learn of a commotion and the presence of police. In nearby Rowan Road, where the Whyte children spent the remainder of that night with a relative, they were saying even less.

By midnight, the prefabs at Rosehill were wrapped in darkness but the lights burned late in the farmhouse as detectives worked on. In the early hours of Tuesday, Chief Detective Inspector William Duncan, head of CID, told the waiting pressmen:

> Mrs Elizabeth Stewart or Whyte (43), housewife, Rosehill Farmhouse, 12 Blackthorn Crescent, Aberdeen, was admitted to the Royal Infirmary last night, between 9 and 10, suffering from gunshot wounds from which she subsequently died. A man is detained in the Royal Infirmary suffering from injuries arising out of the incident which occurred at the farmhouse.

The casualty was her husband, William, who had been found unconscious outside the farmhouse with a suspected fractured skull. Police kept a vigil at his bedside. Whyte was on the danger list. He had shot his wife twice with a shotgun. He had fired the first shot as Mrs Whyte fled upstairs, probably to warn her two eldest sons in their bedroom. The terrified woman reached the first landing but her enraged husband took aim and fired again. Mrs Whyte collapsed, dying.

This shooting caused a sensation in Aberdeen and the northeast as it became the third case of homicide in the city that year. In May, a man was arrested on a charge of murdering a trawl fisherman in the dockland area. That charge was reduced to culpable homicide but, eventually, on instructions from the Crown Office, the proceedings were dropped. And, in July, as we have seen, Eric Stephen strangled his wife.

Mrs Whyte, described by a neighbour as a nice, quiet woman, had bred husky dogs at Rosehill. The family, who had stayed there for three years, had their roots in Buchan. When Chief Inspector Duncan returned to the farm in the daylight, he was accompanied by Chief Constable Alexander Matheson. In charge of the case was Detective Inspector Harry Halcrow. It was left to Robert Whyte, the eldest son, to sum up the feelings of the motherless family. He said that they had only horrible memories, which they wanted to forget. 'I am determined that we stick together,' he added. 'Whatever happens I don't want my brothers and sister to be separated.' He vowed they would leave to the city and never return. In the coming days, relatives rallied round the grief-stricken siblings. In its report of the shooting, the *Scottish Daily Express* said that the accused had recently left a mental hospital of his own accord.

On Wednesday 3 September, the Marquess of Huntly, Chieftain of the Aboyne Games, walked across a sun-splashed arena for the games' opening ceremony. Meanwhile, at Aberdeen Royal Infirmary, two sleek black police patrol cars drew into the grounds at Foresterhill. From an open window in a nearby block, a radio played the popular tune, 'Music While You Work'. One car parked in the nearby staff car park while the other halted at the staff entrance. Two detectives and two uniformed policemen entered the hospital. Half an hour later, they re-appeared with Whyte, who was wearing a white shirt, with the sleeves rolled up, and Lovat green trousers. He walked with a limp but managed to get into the car unaided. The police activity went unnoticed by off-duty nurses and Whyte was driven off. Later that day, he made a one-minute appearance before the sheriff at Aberdeen Sheriff Court. He was remanded in custody for further examination.

On Friday 3 October, the public benches were almost empty when Whyte, who gave his full name as William McLennan Whyte, followed wife-strangler Eric Stephen into the dock at their High Court Pleading Diet. Whyte, dressed all in green – trousers, shirt and tie – was the first man in Aberdeen to face a capital charge of murder under the Homicide Act (1957). He cocked his head to one side as the charge was read. For one brief moment, he shook his head in disbelief. His agent, Mr H J G Connochie, advocate, lodged a plea in bar of trial on the grounds that, when the alleged crime was said to have been committed, the accused was then, and still was at that time, insane and unfit either to plead or instruct his defence. Sheriff Hamilton ruled that the case be continued to the High Court.

Before the start of Eric Stephen's High Court trial eleven days later, Whyte was found insane and unfit to plead. He sat unmoved during the twenty-minute hearing which was mostly taken up by medical experts. Lord Wheatley ordered him to be detained indefinitely.

Blood-soaked Rosehill Farmhouse and the prefabs are history. The street names, Blackthorn, Rowan, Plane Tree and Laburnum survive, but a trim, terraced housing scheme has replaced what once stood there.

A NOTE ON THE HOMICIDE ACT (1957)

At the beginning of the nineteenth century, there were more than 200 capital crimes, ranging from shoplifting to treason. Hanging under-sixteens in Britain was finally stopped in 1908 and, in 1933, under-eighteens were no longer hanged. Instead, they were to be detained during His Majesty's pleasure. In March 1957, parliament passed the 1957 Homicide Act, which limited capital murder to five offences, namely: murder while carrying out theft; murder by shooting or as the result of an explosion; murder while resisting arrest or during an escape; murder of a police or prison officer; and the committing of two murders on separate occasions.

14

DEAD MAN WAKING

1960

Birdsong hung in the air above Aberdeen's Broad Hill, the hillock once known as the *Cunningar*, an old Scots word meaning 'rabbit warren'. Here, in bygone times, the townsfolk used to hunt rabbits for food. On the playing field below the eastern slope, cricketers neared the final over as unsuspecting couples strolled on the links and teenage girls headed for the Beach Ballroom.

But death did not take a holiday on the afternoon of Saturday 21 May 1960. Uniformed constables stood guard round the crown of the hill as their colleagues probed for clues in a grassy hollow a few yards from the railings of the Trinity Cemetery to the west and within sight of Gallow Hill. Just after 5 p.m., two schoolgirls had stumbled upon the brutal murder of fish worker Margaret Wilkinson (32), known to her friends as 'Margo'.

The second youngest daughter of a family of seven, Margo had left home in Sandilands Drive at 7.30 a.m. to go to work at a fish merchant's in South Esplanade West and she never returned. That afternoon, Margo was drinking in the Aberdeen Arms public house in West North Street when two young men entered. Former regular soldier John Douglas Leslie (23), a building labourer, and a trawlerman friend, Harold Riley were on a pub crawl and had visited various hostelries before landing at the 'Hairy Bar', the age-old nickname given to the pub. Leslie was introduced to Margo by his companion and, after buying some beer and wine, the trio left by taxi for the Broad Hill at 2.30 p.m. The taxi dropped them off in nearby Golf Road and they climbed the hill. They sat and drank for some time and, after Riley had had sex with Margo, he left on his own.

After the schoolgirls had raised the alarm at 5.15 p.m., police found Margo's body in the hollow. She was dressed in a camel coat and black dress. She was also wearing black Wellington boots with the tops turned down in true fish-worker style. Her face was bloodstained and she had been strangled. The killer had left behind a bit of broken boot lace.

The tragedy shocked her family and neighbours. Margo, who was about five feet tall, was described as friendly and cheerful. Less than twenty-four hours after the grim discovery, Chief Inspector William Duncan, head of Aberdeen CID, announced that a man had been arrested in connection with her death and would appear at the city's Sheriff Court on the Monday.

In the early hours of Sunday the 22nd, Chief Inspector Duncan and Detective Inspector Harry Halcrow had gone to Leslie's home at 48 Manor Avenue. When cautioned and charged, he replied, 'I strangled her with my boot lace.' But when he appeared at the High Court in Aberdeen on 19 July 1960, Leslie denied murdering Margo. Day one of the two-day trial was charged with high drama, beginning with the eye-witness accounts from the two girls on the Broad Hill and ending with the accused entering the witness box.

The only light relief came when Lord Kilbrandon, the judge, rebuked the public for laughing when a witness referred to the aforementioned 'Hairy Bar'. In his guide to city pubs, Archibald Hopkin wrote that this nickname had been the subject of some fanciful conjecture. The Aberdeen Arms, which closed in 1972, once bordered an area used for stabling and farmers had frequented the premises to barter for horsehair, used in stuffing mattresses and pillows.

The voices of ten-year-olds Alison Laing and Patricia Smith were reduced to a whisper as they relived the grim ordeal of what they saw on the hill. Their evidence was so inaudible that they were asked to repeat it for the benefit of the presiding judge.

Alison, wearing a summer dress and blue jacket, stood beside the jury while recounting events. When she and her friend had reached the top of the hill, they saw a man and woman lying down outside the cemetery railings. The man was on top of the woman and appeared to be tugging with both hands at something round her neck.

Mr V D Skae, prosecuting, asked, 'Could you see what he was tugging at?' Alison shook her head but added, 'He got off, knelt down and then seemed to be doing something to his laces in his shoes.' She said that the man appeared to be shaking the woman's head against the ground. He sat down and seemed to pull her skirt up. Moments later, he fled down the hill, stumbling and falling to his knees as he went. The man had ginger hair and was dressed in a sports jacket and tight blue jeans. She had later picked out Leslie from a line-up at the police station. For good measure, she identified Leslie in the dock.

Defence counsel, Mr C H Johnston QC, asked Alison only one question, 'Did Leslie appear to be drunk or ill as he went down the hill?' She whispered that she thought he was drunk. Patricia Smith, smart in a pleated tartan skirt, white blouse and blue blazer, told how she saw Leslie do 'something' with the woman's neck. Leslie then tied his laces before going downhill. He slipped as he went and appeared to be drunk, added the fair-haired lass. After Leslie left the scene, Patricia went to get help for the woman. Asked why by the prosecution, she replied softly, 'She never moved.'

Another Crown witness was the accused's ex-girlfriend, a teenager who said her parents had not approved of their friendship but that the couple had still managed to meet. She was working in a city store at around 5.30 p.m. on the day of the murder when Leslie, who was crying and in a drunken condition, blurted out that he had murdered a woman. A post-mortem showed that the deceased had minor abrasions on her forehead, temple and chin consistent with being punched. There were double ligature marks on the front of her neck. Three bits of shoelace handed over by police fitted the marks exactly, said Dr William Hendry, police surgeon. Strangulation had been the cause of her death.

The accused's mother, Mrs Christina Leslie (53), said that, before joining the army, Leslie had been a good son. But, after three years' service, he had changed. He had served with the Gordon Highlanders in Cyprus during the troubles there and might have become embittered when a number of his comrades were burned to death in a forest fire started by EOKA terrorists in 1956. (The EOKA, a movement for the liberation of Cyprus from Britain, were particularly active in the 1950s and again in the 1970s.) When drunk, her son became upset and a row usually followed. He was the sort of person who, having taken drink, acted in a dangerous way if aggravated. She told the defence counsel he did not like being 'preached at'. He also suffered from depression and, on one occasion, she arrived home to find the gas cooker turned on and her son asleep in bed.

On the Saturday morning before the murder, Leslie had been quite normal. He had left the house before 11 a.m. and had not returned until 6.20 p.m. He was drunk which was unusual for him at that time of the day. His mother had left him alone in the house and, when she came back at 9.30 p.m., he was in bed. Asked by Mr Johnston how her son had looked, she replied, 'My impression was that he was like a dead man waking. His eyes seemed to be fixed in his head staring. He was pure white. I did not speak to him and he did not speak to me.'

Leslie, a slight, short figure in a blue suit and light-blue pullover, had shown scant emotion while hearing the evidence. Now it was his turn in the witness box and the courtroom became hushed as he described how he killed Margo Wilkinson. He admitted strangling her but denied murder. Before the pub crawl, he had had £4 but, by the end of the afternoon, he was left with loose change – 1s 6¹/₂d in all. Apart from the booze they had consumed on the Broad Hill, he and Riley had earlier downed a mixture of beer, cider and wine. He had been present when sex between his companion and Margo Wilkinson had taken place on the hill. Afterwards, they had all fallen asleep and he had awakened to find himself alone with her. 'Was she alive or dead?', asked Mr Johnston. He replied, 'She was alive.'

When Margo had wakened up, she began to cry. Leslie had asked her what was wrong. She told him that she was afraid because her brothers might beat if she arrived home at a late hour. Leslie said that he had tried to comfort her. He had lain down beside her on the grass and had spoken soothing words to make her stop crying. It did not seem to work. Leslie, when asked what was the next thing he remembered, hesitated before replying, 'I killed her. I strangled her, sir.'

There had been no reason for him to do this. They had not quarrelled and had been speaking naturally and calmly up until that point. He told Lord Kilbrandon he remembered strangling her. Asked by Mr Johnston if he had experienced any feeling of anger when doing this, Leslie replied, 'I suppose I was mixed up inside.'

After he had been demobbed from the army in 1958, he had had bouts of depression and had attempted suicide by slashing his arm with a razor and, later, by gas poisoning. Leslie, cross-examined by the prosecution, denied that the slashes were 'trifling' and that he had invented the gassing incident. He refuted Mr Skae's claim that he had lost his temper when the victim repulsed his advances. Leslie said that he did not know why he had strangled Margo Wilkinson but he was sure he had not done so in anger at being repulsed. A psychiatrist told the court that Leslie did not suffer from any mental abnormality. He showed a lack of a sense of values and a lack of proper maturity, a condition that could not be treated by psychiatrists. By reason of the effect of alcohol, Leslie was quite capable of causing the death of a woman and being unable to remember what had happened.

Next day, Leslie sat impassively as Mr Johnston tried to convince the jury of nine women and six men that the 'horrid concoction'

123

of drink he had consumed might have resulted in the accused suffering a diminished sense of responsibility. He was not fully responsible for his actions at the time and they should return a verdict of culpable homicide. But his plea failed. The jury found Leslie guilty of what Lord Kilbrandon described as 'a terribly serious and terribly sordid crime'. The case, he commented, was perhaps unique in that, apart from the accused's admission, the murder had been witnessed by two ten-year-old girls.

Leslie swallowed hard when the judge sentenced him to life imprisonment. Then he turned quickly between two white-gloved policemen and walked downstairs from the dock. In the cell below the courthouse, Leslie, still betraying no emotion, told his family he would serve his time. His mother and the rest of the family had clung to the hope that the murder charge would have been reduced. Margo's mother, Mrs Catherine Wilkinson (63), a widow for twelve years, commented, 'He got what he deserved. My daughter had a terrible death.'

15

MURDER WITHOUT MOTIVE

1964

Mild-mannered Jim Millsom (23), known to his family and friends as 'Junior', had everything to live for. The young painter had three bonnie bairns, aged from fifteen months to four years, and his wife, Maureen (25), was expecting another. The Millsoms had been living with Jim's parents in Stewart Terrace, Northfield, and were due to move into their new home. But his life was cruelly cut short when he and a pal went for a beer and a game of darts at a busy central pub. Pay day was Thursday and they often popped into Bill's Bar in Market Street on Thursdays on the way home from work.

Unfortunately, when they stepped into the brightly-lit premises, on 22 October 1964, they were at the wrong place at the wrong time. For 'Junior' Millsom was brutally stabbed by a complete stranger in a murder without motive and his workmate had the traumatic experience of finding him dead. Top cops, headed by Chief Constable William Smith, arrived at the pub soon after Millsom's body had been removed to Aberdeen Royal Infirmary, Woolmanhill. A crowd of about sixty had pressed forward as the dead man was stretchered to a waiting ambulance. Inside the pub, detectives interviewed staff as a police photographer and forensic expert went about their business.

In the early hours of Friday the 23rd, Chief Detective Inspector Harry Halcrow confirmed that they were investigating a man's death. Reporters knew that a man had been stabbed. Later that day, they were told the name of his alleged killer. Bachelor James

Connor Smith (22), a labourer, made a brief appearance at Aberdeen Sheriff Court charged with murder. The forlorn figure of Smith's father sat hunched on a bench as his son, his trousers held up by string, was led before Sheriff Aikman Smith. Afterwards, the fiscal said Smith had been kept in custody for further inquiries. Smith's address was given as Duff Street, off Park Street.

The Millsom children played happily at their grandparents' home, unaware of the tragedy. Their mother was heart-broken. Her mother-in-law revealed that the couple had been due to sign for a new council house that same day. Before the turn of the year, Mrs Millsom had given birth to a baby boy and her young family had moved into their new home in Rowan Road.

On Christmas Eve, Smith, small and slightly-built with dark brown curly hair, appeared at a High Court Pleading Diet in the Sheriff Court. He denied murder by stabbing James Millsom on the body, leg and hand with a knife. The youngest of a family of three, he spoke only to acknowledge his name and to plead. He was sent to the High Court for sentence early in the New Year. Fifty-eight witnesses, including sixteen police officers and a retired police sergeant, were cited to give evidence for the prosecution. On Tuesday 5 January 1965, the first day of the three-day trial, a queue had formed outside the courthouse before 9 a.m.

Bill's Bar (which has since acquired a new name) was comprised of a public bar, a snug bar called The Snuggery and a downstairs lounge, The Looking Glass. It had two entrances – from Market Street and from Adelphi Lane, which runs from Market Street to the Adelphi, which was built in 1815 on the cropped summit of St Katherine's Hill, a former landmark mentioned in the Aberdeen witchcraft trials.

On the fateful day, Millsom and his workmate, Neil Howie (28), also a painter, had finished work at 4.30 p.m. and had arranged to meet up half an hour later in Market Street. Howie, of Abbey Place, Torry, who had known the deceased for eighteen months, described him as 'an easy-going chap'. After linking up again, the pair went into Bill's Bar. In the course of the evening, they were joined for a game of darts by another colleague, Bob McKenzie (29), and two other men. They all had a drink together before these two other men left at about 7 p.m. McKenzie stayed in the company of Millsom and Howie. McKenzie said that Millsom had been drinking beer.

Howie told Mr J H McLuskey QC, advocate-depute leading for the Crown, that he did not know the accused, Smith, and nor had he seen him in the pub before. Millsom left the bar to go to the toilet at around 9 p.m. That was the last time Howie had seen him alive. Moments later, an elderly man, a stranger, came up to Howie and McKenzie and told them that something was wrong and that they should go to the gents' toilet. Howie and McKenzie headed for the toilet. Mr McLuskey asked, 'Did you see anyone enter or leave the toilet?' and Howie replied, 'No. No one at all.' Then his voice dropped to a hoarse whisper. 'I found Jim lying on the floor. He was dead.' Millsom's clothing was disarranged and he was bleeding profusely as he lay on his back. Howie pulled up his dead friend's jersey and shirt and saw two small wounds in the region of the heart. There had been no trace of a pulse, he added. As he knelt to support his friend's head, a few people looked into the room. Howie said that he did not know any of them.

There was a moment of drama as Howie described how he had gone with his friend in the ambulance to Woolmanhill Hospital. Suddenly his face grew pale and his voice became faint, then faltered. He asked permission to sit down in the witness box. He sat with his head in his hands and then, after sipping some water, he continued giving evidence. He told Mr McLuskey that Millsom, who had drunk five or six beers, was not the argumentative type. On the night he died, he was his normal, easy-going self. At this point, Lord Migdale ordered a short break to allow Howie to recover before Dr Robert Taylor, defending, began his cross-examination.

After a fifteen-minute break, Howie returned to the box to

confirm that there had been no quarrel between Millsom and the accused. McKenzie, a labourer, said the toilet was empty, apart from their friend's body and he, too, had not seen anybody leave. Because of the position of Millsom's body – his head was in the water channel and his legs folded back – McKenzie thought he had been struck and the force had caused him to hit the wall. There was nothing to indicate what had happened to Millsom until they saw the stab wounds on his chest. Medical evidence showed that Millsom had been stabbed through the heart. Wounds to his left hand indicated how he had tried to ward off the cowardly and vicious attack.

The murder weapon was a butcher's boning knife. It had a wooden handle and a seven-inch-long blade. Police found the knife in a locked passage half-way up Adelphi Lane. It had been thrown from the lane, bounced off a wall and landed on a doorstep. A knife had been given to Smith on the afternoon of the 22nd. He was told to get rid of it but he decided it might be handy for skinning dogfish at the market. During the trial, the jury of eight men and seven women heard several more eye-witness accounts from staff and customers in the bar about a knife.

Smith was a patron of the snug bar, where he was known as 'Smithy', and, on the fateful evening, he had been drinking there with some acquaintances. He caught his jacket on a chair and part-time barman Leslie Adams spotted the handle of a knife sticking out of the back of his trousers. Charles Robertson (23), a labourer who knew Smith, told a hushed court of seeing the accused stumble from the toilet with a bloodstained knife in his grasp and blood on his face, hands and shirt.

Earlier in the day Smith had been the worse for drink and had taken 'goof pills'. When Robertson joined Smith and others in the Snuggery, the accused was flashing a knife with a handkerchief wrapped round its handle. Smith was asked to hand over the knife but refused. He stuck it back in his trousers with the handkerchief round the blade. At 9.30 p.m., Robertson went to the toilet upstairs near the Market Street entrance.

Smith staggered out of the toilet. Robertson had recognised the knife in Smith's possession as the same one he had had in the snug bar. Robertson told a hushed court: 'The knife was covered in blood. There was some blood on the handkerchief, as well, and blood on his face, hands and shirt. He was in a terrible state.' He said that Smith had blurted out, 'I have stabbed the guy. What am I going to do?' He asked to swap shirts with Robertson but he refused.

Constable Norman Gavin (42) took the names and addresses of people as they filed out of the pub. Each person was asked if they knew anything of what had happened. Most shook their heads and said they didn't. But Smith, who was drunk and argumentative, told him, 'Some b*****d's got a kickin'. It's only a common assault.' At the time, Constable Gavin knew there had been a stabbing but he did not know that the victim was dead. Smith's response indicated to him that he knew nothing of the crime.

Robertson and Tom Harper (23), a labourer who had been friends with Smith for a number of years, left the premises with him after giving their details to the police. Harper had earlier failed to persuade his chum to surrender the knife before the killing. Another witness said that Smith had turned nasty when they had tried to take it away from him. But, after the stabbing, Smith lost his nerve. In the Looking Glass, he told newly-wed Ruby Livingston what he had done and said he'd 'get hung'. Smith then sat alone and frightened at a corner table. Her husband, Charles, remembered how a shaken Smith came over to them and said, 'I've just done a boy.'

Allan Mitchell (20) had been standing at the bar in the Snuggery when his friend Smith told him, 'There's a bloke lying dead in the lavatory.' Mitchell, a trawlerman, went to check. He later saw Smith in the Looking Glass. Smith raised his finger to his lips as if to say, 'Keep quiet.' When Harper left Smith and Robertson at the corner of Union Street and Union Terrace, Smith pleaded, 'Don't leave us.' Robertson and Smith retraced their footsteps in

Union Street. At the Regal Cinema, within a shout of Lodge Walk, Robertson advised, 'If you know anything about it, you'd better give yourself up to the police.'

Smith took his friend's advice but, when he walked into the public inquiry office at the police headquarters, he was in a truculent mood. Constable Richard Cormack (33) was talking to a woman at the front desk when Smith barged in and began to shout for attention. Asked what he wanted, Smith replied, 'There was a stabbing in the Snuggery tonight. I had a knife. I was showing it to some of the boys and I threw it on the floor.' Constable Cormack took Smith to the CID room where a detective asked if his clothes could be examined. Smith agreed at first, then asked for a solicitor to be called.

Before Mr A J G ('Gully') Taylor, a well-known city advocate arrived, Smith told the detective, 'I went into a lavatory and saw a boy lying there stabbed.' When Smith handed his clothes over for forensic tests he said detectives would find blood on the soles of his boots, as there had been blood on the floor of the toilet. Detective Sergeant Alistair Smith, a member of the force's identification branch, thought that Smith was slightly befuddled by alcohol when he saw him at 1.45 a.m. on the 23rd. He found traces of blood on the accused's boots, jacket and trousers. His left hand was also bloodstained.

Detective Sergeant Smith, an expert in the identification of textile fibres, told the High Court that he had found similar fibres on the murder weapon and the accused's jacket. Grey cotton fibres stuck to the haft of the knife, which had been found off Adelphi Lane, matched sample fibres taken from the pockets of Smith's suit. A shudder ran through the courtroom when the detective identified the clothes worn by Millsom on the night of the murder. The jacket, jersey, shirt and trousers were caked with dried blood. Slashes in the material bore testament to the ferocity of the attack.

James Connor Smith did not go into the witness box and his counsel did not lead any evidence. In their addresses to the jury

130

both the prosecution and the defence suggested that it was a crime without motive. The advocate-depute did not think the jury would be satisfied that the accused was so incapacitated by drink as to reduce the crime of murder to a lesser charge. Mr McLuskey asked them 'firmly to reject' any suggestion that the charge should be reduced. The evidence against Smith was overwhelming. Pointers to his guilt included: his possession of the knife before and after the crime; forensic evidence regarding his bloodstained clothing and the fibres on the handle of the murder weapon; and his appearance at the material time and particularly, afterwards, when he was actually frightened.

Smith's counsel, Mr Taylor, said that there were two unusual features about the case. No witnesses saw Smith stabbing the deceased, struggling with him or even quarrelling with him before-hand. And Smith had absolutely no motive for killing Millsom. Robbery was certainly not the motive for the sum of £12. 3s $7\frac{1}{2}$d was found on the deceased. If Smith did the deed, he added, then the proper verdict was culpable homicide.

In summing up, Lord Migdale said that the mere taking of drink, even to a considerable extent, was not enough to bring in a verdict of culpable homicide. The jury had to be satisfied that Smith was so drunk that he did not have the intention – and was unable to form the intention – to kill or inflict serious injury. It took the jury fifty-five minutes to find Smith guilty of murder by a majority verdict. Smith, pale and standing erect, betrayed no emotion as Lord Migdale sentenced him to life imprisonment.

In his cell below the court, Smith had a brief meeting with his father, who had sat in the public benches throughout the trial. Afterwards Mr Smith went off to break the news to his wife. In his youth he had been a boxer and the idea of using a knife against anyone would have repelled him.

James Connor Smith had been born and educated in the High-lands. The family moved to Aberdeen where he had finished his education before picking up a number of mundane jobs. Smith, puffing a cigarette, glared at press photographers as he was escorted to a prison van behind the courthouse. He was on his way to a thirteen-year stretch, part of which he served in the Barlinnie Special Unit, designed to deal with problem prisoners such as Jimmy Boyle, the convicted Glasgow murderer turned author and sculptor, now living on the French Riviera.

But the last word remained with Millsom's father-in-law, George Duthie, who, on being asked by the *Press and Journal* to comment on the verdict, replied bitterly, 'Smith got a life sentence, but my daughter got worse, being left alone with four fatherless children.'

MURDERS IN SCOTLAND

The Swinging Sixties spawned a spate of killings in and around Aberdeen. Of the 200 or so murders committed in Scotland, only ten involved women, one of whom was acquitted. At the end of the decade a sordid murder trial at the High Court in Aberdeen became the centre of worldwide attention. On 2 December 1968, the so-called 'trial of the century' ended after ten days with Sheila Garvie and her lover, Brian Tevendale, being jailed for life for the murder of her wealthy farmer husband who had vanished the previous May. Max Garvie's decomposed body was found in an underground tunnel at Lauriston Castle, some miles from his Laurencekirk farm where he was shot.

16

BOTTLE PARTY

1964

March roared in like a lion. The third month of 1965 was in the icy grip of winter with drivers battling blizzards and snow-clogged roads. There was cold comfort at the High Court sitting in Aberdeen where Barbara Torliefson, a kenspeckle figure in the city, took centre stage in a grisly murder trial. Mrs Torliefson, her blonde hair tied in a top-knot, smiled as she was escorted by three policewomen to the back door of the courthouse across an ice-glazed yard.

But there was no room for laughter as the jury of eight women and seven men heard of the horrific injuries she inflicted on a man who took her to his home in the East End of the city. It ended in Charlie Brown (51) drowning in his own blood in the living room of his flat in a four-storey tenement above a bookmaker's shop in East North Street. Torliefson denied murdering Brown and lodged a special plea of self-defence, claiming she had been assaulted by her host. The prosecution alleged she struck him repeatedly on the face with a bottle or similar instrument and thrust the neck of a broken bottle or similar instrument into his open mouth.

The day of the killing, Saturday, 12 December 1964 – eight days after the accused's thirty-eighth birthday – had been a day of wine and no roses for Torliefson and her boozy friends. Wine had been downed out of a bottle at the back of Castlehill, which had been dominated by a former army barracks until it was demolished the following year. One of those at the alfresco drinking session was Torliefson's brother, Tom Wilson (42), who said his sister had taken a good drink. Around tea time, Mrs Catherine Mutten, who lived in King Street, had seen Torliefson and Charlie Brown walk arm-in-arm up East North Street and go into No. 13. The couple had met only once before – two years previously a friend of the accused had taken Torliefson to Brown's house. Now a chance encounter in the street would have tragic consequences for them both.

Brown was obviously not a man to be trifled with. Mutten, who had known him for twelve years, said that, when he was 'in his cups', he would turn nasty and he would lash out at anybody. 'He went off his head and foamed at the mouth,' she said. Wisely, she would give him a wide berth on these occasions. The court later heard that Brown had been hauled before the police court several times over the years to face charges of assault, malicious mischief and breach of the peace. There never seemed to have been a dull moment in Charlie Brown's second-floor flat. Neighbours had complained regularly of rowdy behaviour, noise and undesirable women.

On that fateful Saturday night, neighbours were disturbed by shouts and the thud of furniture being overturned. James Davidson (28) heard what sounded like a bucket being dropped in the street and he decided to see what was going on. He looked out of his window and saw a white enamel pail on the carriageway. Torliefson was leaning on the windowsill of Brown's flat and shouting to passers-by, 'Get a policeman. There's a man dying in here!' Her cries were ignored by them. Davidson, however, decided to investigate. He went to Brown's door. It was locked and when he peered through the letter-box he saw a bloodstained Brown sprawled in a pool of blood on the floor.

Davidson hurried off to fetch two policemen, Constables Alex Falconer and Eric Munro, who were on duty at the corner of King Street and West North Street. The living room at No. 13 was in a shambolic state with the floors and walls splattered with dried blood. Furniture had been tipped over and shards of a broken bottle littered the floor. Torliefson asked neighbour Frank Ritchie (57) for a cigarette and he asked, 'What have you been doing Barbara?' She told him, 'He asked for it. He tried to take advantage of me.' Torliefson told police she had hit Brown – she didn't know with what – when he had tried to strangle her.

Two detectives, who had been present at Brown's post-mortem, said wounds in the floor of his mouth fitted the jagged points of the neck of a broken wine bottle in the flat. Medical evidence showed that Brown had drowned in his own blood. Dr William Hendry said that blood from the deceased's injuries had blocked his lower air passages. If Brown had been conscious, this would probably not have happened. The doctor counted nineteen lacerations to the man's face and head and said that these had probably been inflicted during the fierce struggle between the pair. Injuries to the accused were minimal.

In her evidence, Torliefson said she had accepted Brown's invitation to go for a drink in his flat. They had shared the bottle of wine Brown had put on the table. After they had drunk it, he went out for a second bottle which they also consumed. After that, Brown began dancing and Torliefson also did a few steps. But she claimed that the bottle party turned sour when her host had ordered her to come to bed with him.

Torliefson said she would go for another bottle of wine but, as she made to leave, Brown attacked her from behind. He forced her to the floor and had his hands tight round her throat. In the violent struggle that followed, Brown reached for a wine bottle. Torliefson managed to wrench it from him and struck him in the face with it to get him off her. 'I kept battering, battering and battering,' she said. Torliefson denied she had lost her temper and thrust the jagged bottleneck down his throat.

In his address to the jury, Mr Ewan Stewart, advocate-depute, said that the accused's irregular lifestyle had emerged from the evidence. It was a brutal and vicious assault on an unfortunate man, a man of undesirable character, who had himself been involved in violence in the past. Defence counsel Mr Ian Macdonald QC described Torliefson as a pathetic woman and a chronic alcoholic who had committed the crime against a background of drink. He reminded the jury that morals did not have very much to do with the case. The jurors were there to try a very serious charge of murder. It was not a court of morals. Obviously believing that Torliefson had been provoked, the jury found her guilty of culpable homicide. Lord Migdale said he couldn't ignore the fact a man had died at her hands and sentenced her to seven years' imprisonment.

17

BLOOD BROTHERS

1969 AND 1970

It was news that brought a collective sigh of relief in the Granite City. The 'Phantom', the elusive cat burglar who had held Aberdonians in fear and alarm for over nine months, was behind bars at last. But mild-mannered Alexander Stewart's incredible housebreaking spree was only the first episode in what was to become a story that would climax in an orgy of blood. The first murder was perpetrated by Alexander's younger brother, Frank, and that was to be followed by those committed by the erstwhile 'Phantom'. In mid December 1969, Frank, a dangerous loner, battered an elderly night-watchman to death in a quarry. He was detained in Carstairs State Mental Hospital and, within a year of being sent there, he was joined by his brother, Alexander. The 'Phantom' had brutally stabbed two women – one of whom was his estranged wife, Shirley.

The 'Phantom's' fantastic trail of burglaries began on Christmas Day 1956 and continued unchecked until 14 September 1957, when he walked into a police trap. During that period, Stewart (24) was responsible for breaking into almost 100 properties. Aberdeenshire-born Stewart had his first run-in with the law at the age of thirteen and would later be sent to an approved school. The former soldier – he had served with the Royal Artillery in the Middle East before being discharged in 1956 – proved an audacious sneak thief on his return to civvy life. He had the knack of entering property by squeezing or wriggling through an unsecured window. He raided only ground-floor homes, many of which were council properties.

The week before his arrest, the burglar's latest exploits made the front page lead in the *Evening Express* – 'THE PHANTOM AGAIN?'. In the early hours of the Friday 6 September, four homes in Hilton and Ashgrove were broken into. In Hilton Place, a woman disturbed the intruder when she heard a door creak and switched on the light. He fled empty handed. He had no luck either when he entered the home of the future Lord Provost Robert Lennox in Gillespie Crescent. Councillor Lennox phoned the police as the housebreaker made a getaway. Then the city's housing convener, he quipped, 'I knew it wasn't someone after a house at that time of the morning!' In nearby Cadenhead Road, the residents slept undisturbed as two houses were ransacked and a small sum of money stolen.

It turned out that the 'Phantom', who owed his nickname to the press, had been in police sights since July. They were convinced that Alex Stewart was their man but they were not prepared to pounce on him until they felt the circumstances would ensure his coming before a judge. Because of increased police vigilance, the 'Phantom' kept his head down in August but, by September, he had resumed his nocturnal activities. Police officers surrounded the unemployed man's council house, at 13 Kilgour Avenue, and waited. During their vigil, they learned that two houses had been broken into in nearby Harris Drive, Tillydrone. At around 3 a.m., Stewart was apprehended as he slipped inside the common lobby at No. 13. 'All right, fellows,' he told the arresting officers. At the police station, the officers discovered that Stewart's haul included cash, sweets, matches, a fountain pen, cigarettes and a postal order. They also found a pair of women's cashmere gloves which he had worn during the raids. They had been unwittingly loaned to him by a female friend. A search of his bedroom uncovered a number of other stolen items.

Stewart's luck had finally run out and, on 9 October, he appeared in the dock at Aberdeen Sheriff Court when the only time he spoke was to admit ninety-four charges, all but one of which were connected to housebreaking and theft. Stewart pled guilty to fifty-five counts of theft by housebreaking, twenty-five of housebreaking with intent to steal, eleven of attempted housebreaking with intent to steal, one of theft by housebreaking and opening lock-fast places with intent to steal, one of theft and one of driving away a motor cycle in Middlefield Terrace, Aberdeen. The value of the stolen property came to £280 10s 11d (about £4144 in today's money), of which only £18 3s 4d (£266) was recovered.

Stewart, tie-less and dressed in a smart grey raincoat, listened as Mr A L Nixon, prosecuting, said the accused's conduct had caused considerable alarm in Aberdeen, especially in homes where the only male resident was on night shift or there was no man living there. Because of the widespread publicity, Stewart had been dubbed the 'Phantom'. 'In the public interest, I would like to make it clear that he was far from that,' the procurator fiscal said, adding that Stewart was unemployed but he was not prepared to go without and that had been the motive behind his extraordinary series of crimes.

Mr Hugh Cochran, defending, said that, having committed the first two crimes, Stewart had grown in confidence and housebreaking had become a regular part of his life. He was quiet and inoffensive and had cooperated with the police since his arrest. Mr Cochran said, 'I think he is somewhat frightened and deflated now that this stage has arisen. He has expressed his regret at his form of life and tells me he has made up his mind to finish altogether his life of crime.'

Sheriff Aikman Smith, imposing sentence of two years' imprisonment, told Stewart he was a sneak thief who had enjoyed a run of luck. The worst aspect of the case was the alarm caused to elderly people and women living alone. He added, 'I hope you don't think that, because you were given a nickname, you are a romantic figure. You have shown yourself to be, on the whole, a petty criminal.' The Sheriff had considered sending Stewart to the

High Court for sentence. But, because of the accused's age and the fact that the longest-ever jail term he had served was three months, he decided to impose the maximum sentence he could give. 'Aberdeen's "Phantom Burglar" is no more,' commented the three-penny *Evening Express*. The story of the burglar's conviction almost eclipsed the sighting that morning of Russia's satellite, Sputnik, streaking over Edinburgh.

Despite Stewart's vow to keep on the right side of the law, he resumed his life of crime and was in and out of jail over the next few years. A steadying influence entered his life in the shape of Shirley Lonie, an attractive divorcée, whom he wed at Aberdeen Registrar's Office in October 1963. But an intolerable strain was placed on their marriage as Stewart, who had been working as a labourer, reverted to his criminal past, leaving his wife to bring up three young sons whenever he was behind bars.

Stewart was born in the Buchan village of New Pitsligo in December 1932. He was the second oldest of a family of seven. His brother, Frank, was seven years younger. Frank, a bachelor, was a loner who did not make friends easily. He had held down a number of jobs, from van boy to cinema usher, before joining the army on a nine-year engagement. He was medically discharged and for ten years worked as a labourer with a firm of scrap merchants at a former quarry at Persley. It was there, amid the piles of wrecked cars, that Frank Stewart killed one of the few people he trusted.

Christmas 1969 was ten days away and Aberdeen housewives were being tempted with some last-minute gift ideas, ranging from a crystal flower vase at 42s (£2.20) to a double-sized electric blanket at £7. A top city butcher was advertising 5–6lb oven-ready turkeys from 25s (£1.25) to 30s (£1.50) each.

Before midnight on Monday 15 December, Frank Stewart made his regular visit to the yard to chat with night-watchman William Gerrie Thain (73). Stewart (30) wanted to broaden his outlook so he could mix better. In his quest for knowledge, he would pore

141

over encyclopaedias and was especially interested in history. He also enjoyed nothing better than a good detective thriller on television. Stewart looked forward to these 'chin-wags' with Thain who lodged with widow Mary Stuart in a ground-floor tenement flat in Alexander Terrace (which had formerly been called Kilgour Avenue). Thain, known as 'Uncle Bill' to Mrs Stuart and neighbours, was fit for his age. He said he had been a boxing champion in the army and every day he cycled to work – a distinctive figure in a coloured beret with an army pack slung over his back. The old man had worked at the scrap yard for two years and, while on duty, he was not alone as Alsatian dogs also kept guard.

On the fateful night, Stewart had been at the bottle. Thain had regularly warned the loner about his heavy drinking and it would appear he had begun to lecture Stewart on its pitfalls. Despite their friendship, Stewart may have nursed a grievance. He claimed he had been overlooked for the post of night-watchman. In the watchman's hut, a heated argument broke out between the pair and blows were exchanged. Stewart saw red and picked up an iron ladle. He struck the watchman repeatedly, inflicting terrible injuries. He later said, 'I should have ignored him – he was much older than me.' According to his version of events, Stewart said he had acted in self-defence, saying Thain had threatened him with an iron bar. After the brutal killing, he went home to bed. The ladle used to beat 'Uncle Bill' to death became an exhibit in Grampian Police Force's museum collection. At the 9.30 a.m. on Tuesday the 16th, workmen at the yard found Thain's dead body. Less than eight hours later, detectives of the north-eastern Counties Constabulary announced they were investigating a murder and that a man would appear at Aberdeen Sheriff Court.

Late that night, MPs voted overwhelmingly to abolish hanging for good. The result (343 votes to 185) was greeted with loud cheers on all sides of the House. To support his motion to make the abolition permanent, Home Secretary Jim Callaghan said that, so far that year, murders in the United Kingdom were down. In

Scotland, up to 15 December 1969, there had been twenty-five cases of murder known to the police, compared with forty in 1968. Of those twenty-five, eleven were still unresolved, compared to eight in the previous year. The law to end the death penalty had first been passed in 1965 and The House of Lords also accepted that it should be in force indefinitely.

When he appeared at the High Court in Aberdeen on 31 March 1970, Frank Stewart admitted the culpable homicide of the watchman After hearing medical evidence from Dr Andrew M Wyllie and Dr Alexander H Innes, of Cornhill Hospital, Aberdeen, Lord Kissen ruled that Stewart was suffering from a mental disorder within the meaning of the Mental Health (Scotland) Act, 1966, and ordered him to be detained in Carstairs without limit of time.

Within a year, the same doctors returned to the same witness box after Frank's wayward brother, Alexander (now 37), newly released from Peterhead Prison, stabbed his wife and another woman to death in Aberdeen. The jealous husband took his revenge after he had discovered that Shirley Stewart (32) had left him for another man. He had been released from jail four days earlier and was on £5 bail from Aberdeen Sheriff Court on a breach of the peace charge.

At 4 p.m. on a cold October afternoon in 1970, the terrified screams of his wife rang out in Northfield, a council estate in the north of city. She had been stabbed. Shirley, a butcher's shop assistant, stumbled from the premises in Moir Crescent, pursued by her crazed husband. He stabbed her again as she tried to reach the grocer's shop next door and she crumpled in a blood- spattered heap in the shop doorway. As his wife lay dying, Stewart bent over her and said, 'I love you.'

Grocer James Morrison dialled 999 as three fear-stricken youngsters were ushered out of his shop to safety by neighbour Mrs Rene McLellan, who owned the nearby newsagent's. Shirley Stewart was rushed by ambulance to Aberdeen Royal Infirmary but she was found to be dead on arrival. Police found and arrested

Stewart shortly afterwards. Then, three hours after being called to the murder scene at the shop, detectives got another emergency call – this time from someone living within a mile of the murder scene. At tea-time on Monday 19 October, the body of Daphne McWilliam (40), the wife of the man Shirley Stewart had been seeing, was found stabbed on the kitchen floor of her home in Raeden Crescent. Mrs McWilliam, the devoted mother of two teenage children, had been killed by Stewart some hours before he attacked his wife. It was revealed that the killer had telephoned Mrs McWilliam, giving her a false name, and later he had gone to her home.

At the High Court in Aberdeen on 26 January 1971, Stewart, described as a prisoner in Aberdeen, was charged with murdering Mrs McWilliam at her home at 54 Raeden Crescent, by stabbing her repeatedly on the body with a knife or similar instrument and striking her on the head and face with a pan. He was also accused of murdering his wife, Shirley, of Deeside Gardens, by stabbing her repeatedly with knives in the two shops in Moir Crescent. Only two witnesses were called – the above-mentioned Dr Wyllie and Dr Innes. Dr Wyllie (64), physician superintendent at Cornhill Hospital, said Stewart suffered from 'a mental depression with psychopathic personality' and that he was also suicidal. Dr Wyllie, who had researched the accused's family history, told Mr J R Craik, defending, that Stewart had said the background to the offences was his discovery, on being released from prison, that his wife was living with another man. He called on this other man's wife, had an argument or quarrel with her and killed her. Mr Craik asked, 'Did he then go and find his wife who was working in this other man's shop, again had a quarrel with her, fought with her and stabbed her, causing her death?' Dr Wyllie said he believed this to be the case.

Dr Innes, a medical assistant at the hospital, also told the court of two suicide attempts by Stewart in 1969. In March, he had been admitted informally to Kingseat Hospital, Aberdeenshire, after he tried to kill himself by coal gas poisoning. This had been brought on because of depression and marital and financial problems. He ignored medical advice and discharged himself from hospital. In May, he threw himself over a balcony at Craiginches Prison but only fell one floor. Stewart said that he had done this because his wife had not visited him while he was in jail. Mrs Stewart had told a social worker that her husband had assaulted her and the children. She did not contact the police because she was afraid he would kill her. The court also heard that Stewart's brother was in Carstairs for 'a very serious offence'.

After hearing the medical evidence, Lord Cameron accepted the defending counsel's submission that Stewart was unfit to plead to the indictment of double murder because of insanity. The judge, therefore, deserted the diet against Stewart and ordered him to be detained in Carstairs without limit of time. As Alexander Stewart went off to join his brother Frank, who had been a patient there since the previous March, I spoke to their mother, Mrs Joan Stewart (60), in the family home in Alexander Terrace. Soft-spoken Mrs Stewart said, 'I am heartbroken. We cannot believe this could have happened a second time to us.' She defended Alex, claiming, 'He is a good boy really. He did not drink and thought the world of his wife and family.' Of Frank, she said, 'Frank was a different sort and kept himself very much to himself.'

18

DEATH ON DUTY

1977

An hour before midnight on 8 August 1977, a motorist was spotted parking a Jaguar erratically at the foot of Market Street. The car had its rear wheel on the pavement close to the Douglas Hotel, opposite the house where child-killer Big Jim Oliphant had once lodged. Eighteen-year-old Jacqueline Cruickshank and her friends thought that the man at the wheel was drunk. One of them advised him to leave his car and get a taxi. He replied, 'Why the f*** should I when I've got four wheels of my own?' Another passer-by offered to park the Jaguar but the driver remained belligerent. 'Nobody is going to touch my f***ing car. I'll park it myself.'

At that moment, a police car turned into the road, which is so steep that tracer horses were once used to haul loads up the hill. Two other girls flagged down the police car and Sergeant Alan Gordon, of Grampian Police, approached the Jaguar. He raised his hand to tell the driver to stop and then went round to the driver's open window and put his arm inside. He told the driver, 'Would you stop the car. We only want to speak to you.' Witnesses thought that the policeman was trying to switch off the engine.

Constable John Adair, who was with Sergeant Gordon, warned his colleague to get out of the way because he thought the driver was going to take off. The Jaguar, its tyres screeching, sped off up Market Street with the policeman hanging on. He tried to keep up with the speeding vehicle but his feet got dragged from under him and he fell. He then lay unconscious on the road with blood coming from his mouth.

The Jaguar did not stop. Instead, it accelerated up Market Street on the wrong side of the road before swerving into Union Street where it almost collided with traffic. The driver ignored police roadblocks and headed out of the city but, at the Den of Logie, just north of Stonehaven, the car plunged down an embankment. Constable Michael Spence, who had chased the Jaguar, found the driver lying across the front seat, moaning, 'My ribs, my ribs.' His breath smelt strongly of alcohol. Two days later Sergeant Gordon (38), who was married with three children, died in hospital from severe head injuries.

At the High Court in Aberdeen in October, Derek Brown (23), a lorry-driver, of Victoria Road, Aberdeen, pleaded not guilty to murdering Sergeant Gordon. It was alleged that, to avoid arrest, Brown drove his car forward at excessive speed, whereby the policeman grabbed hold of the car or became caught up by it. To dislodge Sergeant Gordon, the charge stated, the accused accelerated and the police officer fell, sustaining fatal injuries. Brown also denied two other charges of driving recklessly in Aberdeen and on the Aberdeen–Stonehaven road on that same night, of driving through two roadblocks and of driving with more than the permitted amount of alcohol in his blood.

In evidence, Jacqueline Cruickshank, of Stockethill Square, Aberdeen, told how the sergeant was 'sort of dragged' along by Brown's car. When the Jaguar turned into Union Street, she thought the traffic lights were at red. Teenager Karen Jackson, of Chattan Place, Aberdeen, told the court she had waved down the police car because she had suspected that the accused was drunk and could have caused somebody injury. Constable Adair could not see how Brown could be unaware of their presence. The accused swore at the sergeant before accelerating up Market Street. The car travelled up the right-hand side before switching to the correct lane and it had been at this point that the sergeant had fallen off. The constable added that Brown had looked drunk and his eyes were glazed. One witness estimated that the car was travelling at 60 m.p.h.

when it 'shot off'. And, according to another eye-witness, Mrs Margaret Esslemont, it was on two wheels as it swung into Union Street. Medical evidence showed that the Sergeant Gordon had died from a skull fracture which was consistent with his head having struck the rear door handle of the Jaguar.

On the second day of the trial, Brown told his defence counsel, Mr Donald Macauley QC, that he had bought the Jaguar four or five weeks before the alleged incident. He admitted he had drunk about six or seven pints of lager during that evening. He was parking in Market Street when he saw a policeman coming across the road and putting his hand on the car bonnet. He claimed, 'As soon as I saw the policeman, I knew I was going to get done for drunk driving and I wanted to try and avoid this.' The policeman had moved away from the front of his car and, as far as he knew, was not in any danger. As he picked up speed, he felt a tug at his shoulder. Brown thought this might be the policeman but he did not think the officer was in any danger of being 'whipped' by the car. He had no intention of injuring or killing the unfortunate man or doing any harm to anyone. He had no idea the sergeant was trapped or clinging to the central pillar of the car door as he drove away. If he had known, he would have stopped. In cross-examination, Mr Hugh Morton QC, advocate-depute, put it to Brown that he had been determined that the police were not going to stop him – no matter what. Brown replied, 'That's right. I drove off in a blind panic.'

The jury, of eleven women and four men, returned in less than an hour to find Brown guilty of a reduced charge of culpable homicide. He was jailed for eight years and banned from driving for ten years. Brown had changed his plea on two other charges and admitted reckless driving and driving with excess alcohol. The judge, Lord Ross, told Brown that Sergeant Gordon's death had been tragic and wholly unnecessary. It had resulted from Brown drinking to excess and trying to avoid being arrested. He went on, 'I regard an offence of this kind as extremely serious. I have already referred to the extent to which law-abiding members of the community depend on the police and I regard this court as having a duty to impose deterrent sentences.'

The day before Brown stood trial, Lord Ross had warned that the courts would regard any offence, which endangered the life of a police officer in the execution of his duty, with the greatest gravity. Drink was no excuse for violence towards the police and wrongdoers must accept the consequences. The judge made his comments at the High Court in Aberdeen after dealing with two young men who had endangered the lives of police officers by driving stolen cars at them at high speeds. Originally, they had been charged with attempted murder but this was reduced to police assault. They were locked up for a total of eight years and banned from driving for a year.

Sergeant Alan Gordon had been a constable in the force for seventeen years and, in April, four months before his death, he had earned his three stripes. Assaults on police officers in Grampian Region had been growing steadily during the year that Sergeant Gordon died. In the first nine months of 1977, they totalled 186, compared with 165 in the same period the previous year. That represented an increase of more than 12 per cent. Grampian Police Chief Constable Alexander Morrison, commenting on the rising crime rate in the 1970s, had this grim warning for *Evening Express* readers, 'If you impose a worsening crime situation on society for long enough, they will learn to live with it and accept it as the norm, even if that norm meant there were certain areas of the cities in which it was no longer safe to venture at night.'

IN THE LINE OF DUTY

Sergeant Gordon was the first Aberdeen-based bobby to die while investigating a criminal incident in the city. However, there had been earlier police deaths. Three Aberdeen City Police Officers and a member of the City Watchmen, the forerunners of today's force, all died in tragic accidents – either while on duty or while making their way home after a shift.

On 15 June 1909, Constable John Say was cycling on the footpath between the Brig o' Balgownie and the Bridge of Don when he plunged 40 ft down an embankment. He suffered head injuries and died in hospital. He was just 25.

After escorting an injured girl to Aberdeen Royal Infirmary, on 22 August 1915, George Craib, a 40-year-old PC, stumbled and cracked his skull on the ground. He was admitted to the same hospital where he too died.

And Constable Andrew Matthew (40) was cycling home after duty, in the early hours of 26 January 1939, when he was fatally injured in a collision with a car.

The earliest known death of a city lawman is that of Watchman Joseph Collie on 26 October 1835. Collie was heading back to the watch-house during a gale when he was blown into the dock at Waterloo Quay and drowned. His death meant that his family faced destitution and, when the Police Commissioners awarded his widow a miserly pension, John Fyfe, Superintendent of the Watchmen, resigned.

19

DEATH IN THE COVENANTER

1985

The Covenanter Bar took its name from a stirring event in Aberdeen's past, when Montrose's victorious troops defeated the Royalists at the Battle of the Brig o' Dee in June 1639. The spot on Kincorth Hill, where the great soldier directed the attack on the bridge, was long known as 'Covenanters' Fauld'.

The Covenanter, a product of the 1970s, served the post-war council estate of Kincorth where houses rise tier upon tier like a wedding cake. Sadly, the public house, the thriving social centre of Kincorth life with its own country-and-western folk club, later became the site of a major drugs operation in the Aberdeen area and a brutal murder. It first drew unwelcome publicity in 1978, seven years after its opening, when a mob attacked police in the car park after Scotland, the UK's sole representatives in that year's football World Cup in Argentina, lost to Peru in their opening game. Following a lengthy jury trial at Aberdeen Sheriff Court, eleven of the twelve young local men involved in the riot were locked up for a total of seventeen years.

One of the culprits, Brian Beattie (25), a married man, was jailed for four months after being found guilty of breaking the peace. Beattie had had brushes with the law as a juvenile and later became involved in reset and salmon-poaching. But Beattie sought bigger fish to fry and, eight years after the football riot, he was revealed as the mastermind behind a drugs ring that blighted a generation of young people on the Kincorth estate where he was brought up.

This Aberdeen drugs 'baron' was involved in the drugs scene for one reason only – profit – although he claimed he had been addicted to cocaine for eighteen months. With no thought for the young lives that he first manipulated and then destroyed, the former auto electrician used the huge rewards from the illegal trade to provide himself with rich trappings. Beattie preyed on their vulnerability as drug addicts to control his mini-empire. If that did not work, he turned to threats of violence, claiming he was on first-name terms with a notorious Glasgow underworld gang who would deal with anyone who stepped out of line.

Beattie, who sported a heavy black moustache, entered the drugs scene in the early 1980s and, within a few years, seemed untouchable. In 1982, heroin addicts in the city were few in number but, with Beattie's help, their ranks swelled. He set up a protective shield of 'runners', around his drug-dealing. Those involved were too frightened to talk because of their own illegal activities. Because of the protection Beattie was given by his associates, Grampian Police detectives were frustrated in their efforts to bring him to justice.

But, four days before Christmas 1985, the murder of George Ritchie (47) in the pool room of the Covenanter Bar was the catalyst which led to the smashing of the drugs operation. Ritchie, a council car-park attendant, was having a quiet drink with his wife when Beattie's 'minder' stabbed him to death. The killer, Graham Duncan (31), a former oilman, struck after Beattie, who was there playing snooker, pointed Ritchie out to him.

Ritchie held Beattie responsible for ruining the lives of his two sons by supplying them with heroin. In a row outside the Covenanter the previous year, Ritchie had damaged Duncan's car, in the mistaken belief that it belonged to Beattie. In fact, Duncan was behind bars at the time and Beattie was using his car in return for £2500 he had given his 'minder' to buy drugs.

Duncan, nicknamed 'Pot' because of his drug problem, wreaked a terrible revenge. 'Are you the b*****d that smashed my car?' he screamed before he dragged Ritchie from his seat and punched and kicked him. Duncan produced a wicked-looking carving knife from inside his coat. One thrust penetrated Ritchie's spine and paralysed him. Another severed an artery and punctured his lung. (An artist's graphic impression of the horrific attack was published by the *Evening Express* after the trial.) Mrs Ritchie fled from the pool room with its twinkling Christmas lights and multi-hued paper decorations. She ran to a nearby Chinese carry-out from where the police and ambulance were called.

It soon became apparent to detectives that the murder inquiry was drug related. People began to talk – even although many of them were themselves involved in drugs. Beattie was no longer invincible. The High Court trial of Beattie and three others had been due to start in Aberdeen on Monday 17 March 1986. However, after an extra fifty-four witnesses had been cited, it was adjourned until the following day to allow the defence more time to prepare their case. Strict security was in evidence and the media, public and jurors were frisked by police who used metal-detectors. The names and addresses of all those attending the court were carefully recorded.

The trial, before Lord Cowie, was expected to last three weeks with more than 200 witnesses being called by the Crown. But, when the trial resumed on Tuesday the 18th, 'Pot' Duncan admitted murdering Ritchie. Beattie, who had his plea of not guilty to the murder accepted, admitted a list of drug charges between 1982 and 1985. These involved supplying heroin, cocaine, amphetamines and cannabis. He also admitted a number of charges of inciting people to travel to Glasgow and London to buy drugs on his behalf. Most of the drugs offences on the 18-page indictment related to places in the Kincorth area, including the pub in which the murder occurred. Beattie also pled guilty to threatening to break the legs of two men in the Covenanter Bar if they sold drugs.

A third accused, David William Bond (23), admitted assaulting Ritchie, by punching and kicking him, but had his plea of not guilty to murder accepted. He also admitted one charge of supplying cannabis at the Covenanter Bar. Graeme Rose (23) pled guilty to supplying heroin in Kincorth and elsewhere in the city during 1983 and supplying cannabis from Beattie's former home in Kincorth.

Lord Cowie discharged the jury and adjourned the hearing until the following day when Mr Kevin Drummond, advocate-depute, told the court that drugs valued at about £50,000 were involved in the charges to which Beattie had pled guilty. But the figure could have been 'very substantially more' as the value was calculated before the drugs had been cut. Police investigations had revealed that Beattie had funds amounting to £70,000 in various bank and building-society accounts. The court was told that the full extent of Beattie's drugs activity only came to light after Ritchie's murder. The police already had information which suggested his involvement, said Mr Drummond, but the picture which emerged was that he had superimposed his own scheme of operations on to the many existing users, possessors and distributors. Many of their lines of inquiry led back to him. He added, 'Beattie appears to have been using a group of people whom he had established around him and had obtained for himself the major role in the illicit drugs market, in the north-east, but kept himself at arm's length from the daily activities, while exercising a substantial degree of control from the centre.'

But it was the human tragedies associated with his drug deals that proved harrowing in court. Mr Drummond told of one married couple whose lives were ruined by drugs. They spent £20,000 on their addiction, lost their house, cashed insurance policies and also borrowed heavily from relatives. A man told police he was Beattie's best customer, having spent up to £40,000 on heroin from the dealer, including £2000 in one 10-day spell. Duncan's defence counsel, Mr Nicholas Fairbairn QC, described how Duncan himself became one of Beattie's victims. He turned from a successful £34,000-a-year senior toolpusher into a brutal killer. He had just returned from working in Abu Dhabi when Beattie told him his wife was having an affair. Beattie had offered Duncan solace in heroin and his slide into degradation began. 'He became dependent on heroin and, even worse, dependent on Beattie,' said Mr Fairbairn. Because of drugs, he lost his wife, his son and his home. The alienation between Duncan and Beattie was obvious at the High Court sitting, during which they were kept apart in the dock by a policeman.

Lord Cowie handed out the following sentences:

- Graham Duncan was jailed for life for murder.
- Brian Beattie, who would be thirty-three in a week's time, was locked up for seventeen years – one of the toughest sentences handed out to a drugs dealer in Scotland – and fined £19,000.
- David Bond was sent to prison for eighteen months.
- Graeme Rose was jailed for three years.

The judge told Beattie it was quite clear that, over a number of years, he had financed and organised a substantial drug-dealing ring in the Aberdeen area. Lord Cowie went on, 'You have no previous convictions for drugs dealing but that is entirely consistent with you having kept well clear of the day-to-day dealings other than the offence of actually supplying to which you have pled guilty.' Lord Cowie commended the police and the procurator fiscal's department for their work in bringing such a complicated case to court in such a limited time. His hope that they had struck a blow towards eliminating drug dealings in Aberdeen drew a spontaneous burst of applause from the public benches.

Graeme Smith, reporting on the background to the trial in *The Herald*, described how Beattie's career of crime had grown until it finally got to the point where he had cornered the market in heroin in north-east Scotland. The worst hit area was Kincorth where heroin had been virtually unknown until Beattie started dealing in it and the estate became a major drugs black spot. Beattie was dubbed the 'King of Kids', as he recruited impressionable youngsters eager to run errands. Beattie's ambitions grew along with the menace of drugs in society. He progressed from trafficking in cannabis and amphetamines (speed) to heroin and cocaine, both of which made fatter profits. His willing helpers were used to establish a distribution network. Beattie allowed his young runners to take all the risks. They were only too keen to act as couriers to Glasgow and London to collect drugs because it guaranteed their personal supplies.

After setting up a deal by telephone, Beattie would provide the couriers with an air or rail ticket, expenses and a sealed black plastic bag filled with money. The drugs 'baron' had several dealers working for him and each of them specialised in different drugs. His main heroin dealer was understood to have sold around £400 worth of it daily. Beattie alone was understood to have handled £250,000 of drugs in his two main years of heroin dealing. His estimated turnover in heroin, cocaine, speed and cannabis, during the five years before his arrest, was estimated to be more than £500,000.

Beattie's main centre of operations was the pool room in the Covenanter, where users wanting to score would buy a drink and sit at a table. After a deal was arranged with Beattie, one of his runners would leave the premises, returning shortly afterwards with the appropriate drug. Beattie, the 'main man', took no part in physically supplying drugs or in collecting of cash. It was subsequently learned that drugs were hidden in the common lobbies of tenements, waste ground and other safe areas.

On one occasion, police shadowed the Aberdeen couriers to London and back. But the surveillance team had been spotted and the drug deal was aborted. So, when detectives burst into Beattie's house and found a black bag containing almost £10,000, he and his cronies denied all knowledge of it! Beattie later admitted, at the High Court hearing, that the money was to finance a drugs deal. But the police were determined to nail Beattie. His luxury lifestyle of fast cars and foreign holidays ended when the murder inquiry was launched. With Beattie behind bars, his invincibility collapsed and vital witnesses no longer felt threatened.

Two days after the trial ended, 'Pot' Duncan's counsel, Nicholas Fairbairn, praised prison officers for their daily duty in dealing with criminals like Duncan and Beattie. He told the annual conference of the Scottish Prison Officers' Association, 'These were both ruthless characters whom you will have to face every day. That is a fundamental fact which is little appreciated by those who talk about law and order.' Fairbairn, a Tory MP, was speaking before the age of electronic tagging for UK law-breakers and he claimed that there were better alternatives for both punishing and detecting crime.

In Beattie's case a silent bug attached to a bracelet that he could not remove would have enabled police to keep tabs on him. 'This may sound a little like *Star Wars* stuff but I think it would work,' added Mr Fairbairn. 'It would give a way of knowing where someone was all the time. How, for five years, he managed to carry on such a huge trafficking in drugs with so many subsidiary acolytes without being caught is beyond me.' In light of what was said in court about Beattie's elaborate methods to protect himself from prosecution, this was a puzzling statement.

At the end of March, Beattie lodged an appeal against his seventeen-year sentence (sixteen years on the drug offences and one year for breach of the peace) which he claimed was 'excessive'. At the Court of Criminal Appeal in Edinburgh in September, Mr Alastair Cameron QC, acting for Beattie, argued that Lord Cowie, the original trial judge, had no right in law to impose such a hefty sentence. Beattie, he said, had pled guilty on the understanding that the charge of being concerned in the supply of drugs was an 'umbrella charge'. On that basis, the judge should not have imposed separate sentences for the various sub-divisions of the main charge. After Beattie had beaten his own addiction, said Mr Cameron, he had actively tried to work against drugs in Kincorth and had helped form a football team with eight or nine drug addicts in the side.

The Crown maintained that the judge was entitled to impose separate sentences and was not under any obligation to restrict the total sentence. However, on 17 October, Lord Ross, the Lord Justice Clerk, gave the decision of the Appeal Court – Beattie's sentence would be cut by two years. The three judges reduced his sixteen-year sentence to fourteen years, the maximum that could be imposed for such drug offences. However, the extra year on the other charge was upheld.

The smashing of the Kincorth drugs ring helped in the relentless struggle against AIDS and drug-related diseases in Grampian Region. Two years after Beattie was jailed, figures showed the number of hepatitis B sufferers had fallen and doctors were hopeful of a similar drop in the number of AIDS victims. Today the Covenanter Bar has a new name and a new lease of life.

20

THE KILLING OF SISTER JOSIE

1988

Sister Josephine Ogilvie's barbaric death at the hands of a deranged young man shocked a city but the aftermath was an uplifting story of compassion and reconciliation. The bespectacled, silver-haired nun, known affectionately as Sister Josie (59), worked for three years as a religious education adviser in the diocese. Her work took her all over north-east Scotland and the northern isles. She excelled as a teacher and had a wonderful capacity to reach youngsters. People meeting her for the first time found her a little reserved, even shy. But she had a twinkle in her eye and a pawky sense of fun.

Sister Josie, whose order was the Society of the Sacred Heart, was based in the pastoral centre, adjoining St Mary's Roman Catholic Cathedral in Huntly Street. The cathedral, dedicated to St Mary of the Assumption on its completion in 1860, boasts one of the city's tallest spires, which was added, seventeen years later, to mark the church's elevation to cathedral status. Sister Josie shared a first-floor office with her colleague, Father Colin Stewart, the priest who found her body on that sun-splashed but harrowing afternoon of Friday 6 May 1988. The cathedral is only a few paces from busy Union Street and shoppers thronged the pavements.

At 8.30 that morning, Sister Josie had left her home in Dunvegan Avenue, Portlethen, to go to work. She was a dedicated worker and thought nothing of cleaning the floor of her office after a hard day. It was after 2 p.m. when caretaker Felix Graham (68) discovered an odd-looking young man in a corridor in the pastoral centre. The agitated stranger had a silver stud in his left nostril, an earring in his left ear and his hair was cropped to the skull. He spoke with a Liverpool accent. He did not identify himself but his name was Mark Reynolds. Earlier that day he had been seen drinking in at least three bars.

Reynolds told the caretaker he was looking for a 'small nun' and agreed it must be Sister Mary MacDonald, a social worker. He was told she was not there but he insisted on waiting to see her. Reynolds took a chair outside Sister Josie's office and refused to budge, even when ordered to leave by Mr Graham, an ex-amateur boxer of note. Father Stewart disturbed the intruder when he returned to his office and was unable to open the door. It was being forced shut from the other side by Reynolds. The priest suspected a burglar and rushed downstairs to raise the alarm. Both Father Stewart and Mr Graham saw Reynolds hurrying down a fire escape into a backyard, before scrambling over a wall. He was bare-chested and clutching his own and some of Sister Josie's clothes. Ominously, he was covered in blood.

The priest and the caretaker went back upstairs to the office where they were met with a stomach-churning sight. Sister Josie had been brutally murdered. She was half-naked, lying on her back, with her arms outspread, as though crucified. A distressed Father Stewart moved the nun into the recovery position and covered her with his jacket. But Sister Josie was dead. He said a prayer of absolution over her, then waited for the police.

The street was sealed off by police as dog patrols arrived. All possible escape routes from the city were blocked and door-to-door inquiries were mounted in the Crown Street and Dee Street boarding-house area. Because of the killer's Liverpool accent, it was thought he was not local. As Detective Chief Superintendent Norman McCormack, who led the murder inquiry, briefed the media, a statue of St Mary, her hands clasped in prayer, looked down on the cobbled street. Shirt-sleeved undertakers and a uniformed policeman had earlier carried the coffin with the nun's body into a waiting hearse.

Three hours after the killing, police arrested Reynolds. A licensed grocer had identified him from the description given by police and Reynolds was traced to a guest house in Dee Place. He was eating a beef curry while his blood-spattered clothes were in the washing machine in the guest-house kitchen. The food had lain in his room since the night before and he had heated it up on his return from the cathedral. Reynolds told police he had taken LSD and hash but blood tests revealed only cannabis. 'I have done a terrible thing and I don't want to talk about it,' he said. Days later, in Craiginches Prison, he confided to a prison officer, 'I wakened this morning and realised I was a killer – that I had strangled someone.' Sister Josie had put up a brave fight for life and had inflicted scratches on her killer's face.

The crime horrified Aberdeen. Bishop Mario Conti, now the Archbishop of Glasgow and Scotland's leading Catholic Churchman, summed up the feelings of his flock, 'This offends everything we stand for – the sacredness of life, the Church itself and the pastoral centre where Sister Josephine worked so strenuously over the years.' Bishop Conti cancelled a visit to Carfin Grotto in Lanarkshire on Sunday the 8th to attend mass at St Mary's Cathedral. He urged the tearful congregation not to feel resentment and said they should be guided by the Gospel's message of love. 'The eyes of the community are directed upon us,' he said. 'The community must find us at our best.'

On the following day, Reynolds (23), who was described as unemployed, appeared briefly at Aberdeen Sheriff Court charged with the murder of Sister Josie. He was committed for further examination and held in custody. A vigil of prayer took place on the eve of Sister Josie's funeral in the cathedral on Thursday 12 May. There were so many mourners at the Requiem Mass (an estimated 1000) that some had to stand at the back of the church. In his sermon, Bishop Conti said of Sister Josie, 'She had a vision to inculcate the love of God and the service of neighbour in the whole community, starting with children of primary age.'

It was appropriate that pupils from all the city's Catholic schools heard those words. Sister Josie had qualified as a primary school teacher in 1953 before becoming a nun. Among the hosts of floral tributes was a wreath from Father Stewart bearing a touching message, 'Thanks Josie for everything - Colin'. At the graveside in Allenvale Cemetery, Father Stewart led prayers as a small gathering said farewell to a quiet prayerful woman who had been due to take up a new appointment in her native Edinburgh.

The details of the horrific attack and injuries inflicted on Sister Josie were revealed at the High Court in Aberdeen on Monday 23 August when Reynolds pleaded guilty to culpable homicide by reason of diminished responsibility. He admitted that he assaulted Sister Josie, struggled with her, knocked her to the ground, struck her repeatedly on the face, neck and body with his hands, arms and feet, compressed her throat with his hands, jumped and stamped on her body, severed her ear with scissors, bit her, stabbed her and sexually assaulted her. An emotionless Reynolds sat in the dock as Mr Kevin Drummond QC, advocate-depute, said the nun had sustained sixty separate injuries, which included eight broken ribs and a fractured spine. Such injuries were more normally found in victims of road traffic accidents. The cause of death, mercifully at an early stage, was cardiac arrest caused by a major injury to the neck which resulted in a fractured larynx.

The court also heard that Reynolds had moved with his family from Liverpool to Aberdeen in 1978. Before the move to Scotland, the former altar boy had appeared in English juvenile courts for offences of dishonesty. His parents had always shown concern and responsibility for him, said Mr Drummond. At one stage, they had signed documentation to admit him to hospital for treatment for drug abuse. His mother was closely associated with St Mary's and it was she who had introduced him to Sister Mary MacDonald, the social worker he had gone to see on the day of the murder.

Two psychiatrists, who examined Reynolds, recommended that he be detained in Carstairs State Mental Hospital and that an order restricting his discharge should also be made. Dr John Baird, physician superintendent at Carstairs, said it appeared that, since 1982, Reynolds had suffered from schizophrenia and had been treated with anti-psychotic medication. In the opinion of Dr Raymond Antebi, physician superintendent of Glasgow Eastern District, Reynolds had expressed a variety of bizarre beliefs and suffered from thought disorder. Dr Antebi believed that the killing had been the result of a sudden impulse occurring in a mind in chaos. Reynolds had told Dr Antebi that he had been drinking to excess and spent most of the night before the offence awake, smoking cannabis and taking painkillers. The psychiatrist said there seemed to be a history of drug dependence, in particular cannabis and LSD, and agreed drugs might have contributed to his condition but his drug use could also have masked his mental illness.

In response to a question from Lord Cullen, Dr Antebi said he considered Reynolds to be of diminished responsibility rather than insane. That was because he did not appear to be under the influence of a delusion and because he had gone to St Mary's to see a social worker because he was depressed, which indicated reasonable thought. Mr John Morris, for the defence, said the crime was of such a horrific nature that anything he might say in mitigation would sound irrelevant or even offensive. He added, 'It is quite clear he is very ill indeed. The order is in his best interests and those of society.'

Reynolds remained impassive as Lord Cullen sent him to Carstairs without limit of time. After the verdict, newspapers devoted more pages to Reynolds' dark side, describing how he developed an unhealthy obsession in Ninjitsu, an outlawed Japanese martial art. He had owned the ritualistic black uniform, flails and butterfly knives, associated with Ninja warriors of feudal Japan, and liked to watch 'video nasties' featuring their dubious exploits.

But readers also learned of the kindness, compassion and

sympathy shown to Reynolds' devastated family. The dead nun's own rosary was given to his mother on her return to St Mary's. Sister Josie was sadly missed but Bishop Conti told *The Herald* that her colleagues were now able to cope with their duties, having overcome the period of initial shock, horror and upset. But no one was going to be unscarred by the experience, particularly Father Stewart, who had found the nun's body. They had reached the stage where they could talk about what happened without feeling revulsion or fear. There were so many aspects to it. 'The fact that it happened in a sacred place, that it affected a sacred woman, a nun, that it was an act of such violence – it seemed to offend on so many counts,' the Bishop said.

The way the whole community, not just Catholics, had responded was extraordinary. The entire city seemed to share horror, revulsion and grief, he went on. It was practical ecumenism. There were no divisions. The Bishop said Father Stewart had told him, 'People are saying this has shown up the evil in society. It has shown up the good that is in society because of the amount of goodwill.' Bishop Conti said of Reynolds' mother, 'She has suffered very, very greatly over this but has had the courage to come forward and to continue her life as best as she can and to make up in her own life by her prayer and good actions for what she feels her son has done – and that is marvellous.'

21

HOGMANAY HUNT

1964

There had been little cheer that Hogmanay. The news that two young climbers had perished in an avalanche in the Cairngorms had seen to that. However, their other companion had survived after spending twenty-two hours in a tomb of ice and snow. And, in Aberdeen, police were faced with the brutal murder of a semi-invalid. Since having an operation on his foot, shy bachelor Harry Bruce (61), a retired painter, rarely left his snug city-centre flat – except to travel by ambulance to the hospital for further treatment. He had limped since being involved in a road accident during the Second World War. Then, in March 1964, he had had a toe amputated and now he got around at home on a pair of walking sticks.

Mr Bruce relied on his family and a few close friends to bring a morning paper, rolls and groceries. He was known to them and his neighbours as a quiet, kindly man without an enemy in the world. His first-floor flat at 503 George Street was directly above the shop of his brother, Alex, who ran a painter and decorator's business at No. 501. Harry had worked in the shop until his health failed. Banff-born Mr Bruce, the second of a family of eight, was the brother of Baillie Ronald Bruce, a veteran Labour member of Aberdeen Town Council and the city's former senior magistrate.

Harry Bruce kept his flat locked most of the time but, early in the evening of Monday 28 December 1964, someone gained entry and murdered him. The grim find was made at 9 a.m. the next day by members of the deceased's family. His brother-in-law, Charles Gillanders (61), who also lived in George Street, found the flat locked. He got no response when he shouted for Mr Bruce. He fetched his wife, Helen, and when they arrived back at No. 503 the dead man's other sister, Mrs Jean McHardy, was already there. She had a key. Inside, Mr Gillanders found Harry Bruce dead on the floor with gashes on his forehead.

He called the police and, after a post-mortem examination, the city's top detectives moved in. In charge was Detective Chief Inspector Harry Halcrow. Police guarded the stairway to the flat while detectives, with the help of floodlights, made a fingertip search of gutters and rone pipes at the back of the house. They were looking for the murder weapon. All the surrounding back-yards, shelters and outhouses, including cattle pens at the nearby slaughterhouse, were also checked.

Next day Mr Halcrow, accompanied by fiscal Mr A S McNicol, spent some time at the flat. The CID was treating the case as homicide and appealed for anyone who had called at the address, to visit anyone there in the afternoon or evening of Monday, to contact police. They were also interested in hearing about any person who was seen to be bloodstained during the period mentioned. On Hogmanay, as Aberdeen's new festive street lights, which had formerly belonged to London, blazed out, police announced, 'We are now treating this as murder.' Harry Bruce had died of severe head injuries.

As 1964 slipped away, denim-clad policemen spent the day sifting through tons of rubbish at city dumps for possible clues. A posse of special constables was drafted into the hunt, as detectives, armed with questionnaires, called at households in the George Street area. On New Year's Day 1965, Detective Chief Inspector Halcrow revealed that two men had called at 503 George Street at 3.30 p.m. on Monday the 28th and he announced, 'It is urgent, for the furtherance of inquiries, that they contact the police immediately.' He added, 'The hunt will be continued tomorrow, fanning out from the death flat.' All New Year leave for his detectives was cancelled.

On the fourth day of the New Year, detectives knew that the two men, who had called at No 503. on 28 December, went to the house to inquire about a Mr Steele who had formerly lived there. The pair may have also called at the slaughterhouse in Hutcheon Street. Detectives making the door-to-door checks were in a position to show an Identikit picture of one of the men they thought might be able to help in their inquiries. He was aged 22 or 23, 5 feet 8 inches to 5 feet 10 inches tall, broadly built, thin-faced, with fair brushed-back hair and a fresh complexion. He was wearing a zipped khaki jerkin, dark jeans and black Wellington boots.

Events moved on rapidly. By late afternoon, Mr Halcrow announced that two men were at police headquarters assisting the murder team. After giving statements, the men left Lodge Walk in the early hours of the following day. Mr Halcrow and some of his officers had another murder in mind. They had been called to give evidence at the High Court trial of James Connor Smith, who was given life for the Bill's Bar murder. They should have been in the witness room waiting for their turn to give evidence but Lord Migdale granted the prosecuting counsel's request to excuse them from the court-house environs until they were required to go into the witness box.

On 11 January, there was a dramatic development when the CID boss announced that the motive for the murder was robbery. At a special press conference at Lodge Walk, Mr Halcrow revealed that police now wished to interview two other men who were seen leaving the lobby of the two-storeyed building at No. 503 around 6.25 p.m. on 28 December. He added that it was vital for police to interview the men soon and appealed for anyone who knew them or had seen them at the relevant time to come forward.

By the end of the month, the trail was growing colder. True, police had received information that a mystery woman had called at the address in George Street on 28 December but who she was and why she had been there remained a mystery. The photograph of a dark blue reefer jacket, with black shoulder-pads and the word 'Minx' stitched above the right breast, failed to ring bells with any of the public. Police said the jacket had been found during their wide-scale search.

More than 6,500 people were interviewed in house-to-house inquiries in the search for the killer or killers of Harry Bruce. As the files on the case mounted, the murder team moved across Lodge Walk to the former headquarters of the Aberdeenshire Constabulary. The gloomy Victorian building had been vacated in 1963 but I can remember making a personal press call one night in the 1950s as rats scurried along a corridor.

Some sixteen months after Harry Bruce had been found dead, CID boss Harry Halcrow, now promoted to Detective Superintendent, was recalled from leave to take charge of fresh inquiries into the murder. He had talks with Chief Constable William Smith and fiscal Mr A S McNicol but he would only confirm that inquiries were continuing into the murder. At the end of May 1966, the police received information that the murder weapon may have been thrown into the River Don at the Brig o' Balgownie, the fourteenth-century arched bridge immortalised by Byron. Detective Superintendent Halcrow asked Royal Navy divers from South Queensferry to help in a search. Yellow buoys marked out the search area at the 'Black Pot', a 40-foot-deep hole on the upriver side of the bridge. The divers worked from a dinghy with equipment that included a metal-detector. But, after a week-long hunt, they were beaten by the sheer volume of debris on the riverbed.

At the end of the murder inquiry, a report was forwarded to the procurator fiscal but no further action was taken on the grounds of insufficient evidence. The case remains unsolved.

22

DOUBLE IDENTITY

1978

Tall, attractive, with rich brown hair, blue-green eyes and a witty line in conversation, the escort girl had proved charming company. Her dinner dates were two English businessmen, clients of the Edinburgh-based agency for whom she worked. It was common-sense practice for the women on the agency's books not to let slip their real identity to clients or give out phone numbers or home addresses. They would adopt an assumed name for the evening.

That night, in the Treetops Hotel in Springfield Road, Aberdeen, the two executives believed they were dining with a Miss Brenda Adams. They did not know that, during the day, 'Miss Adams' was thirty-two-year-old divorcée Dr Brenda Page, a top genetic scientist at Aberdeen University. Apart from her killer, Dr Page's two dinner companions were the last people to see her alive when she left the luxury hotel to drive home alone through the early morning drizzle on Friday 14 July 1978. It was around 2.30 a.m. when Dr Page left her beige Mini Clubman car in Allan Street, a quiet, cobbled road between Broomhill Road and Irvine Place, and let herself into her ground-floor tenement flat at No. 13, which she shared with her three pet cats.

Twelve hours later, one of Dr Page's colleagues called at No. 13 on urgent business. Unable to get a reply from the doctor, he called on widow Elizabeth Gordon (68), who lived across the hall. Mrs Gordon was on close terms with Brenda, who would drop in on her almost every day to make sure she was all right. They would regularly share a pot of tea and Mrs Gordon was the only person with a spare key to Dr Page's flat. She told the visitor to wait at the door while she checked to see if Dr Page was still asleep. Mrs Gordon thought perhaps Brenda had been working late and was having a lie-in.

The sight that confronted her lived with Mrs Gordon until the day she died. 'I found her in the bedroom,' she said, in tears. 'I saw nothing but blood and hair.' No wonder the poor woman could not bear to live at No. 13 and shortly after the incident, moved to a new home in Bridge of Don. The victim was found sprawled across her bed, fully clothed. Nobody had heard her scream. The grim discovery launched a major murder inquiry headed by Detective Chief Inspector Jim Ritchie. It was established that the victim had died of extensive head injuries and that the flat had been broken into by way of the window of a spare room at the back of the house. It was not known if this was done before or after Dr Page's return. She had not been sexually assaulted.

Detectives thought that the murder weapon, which they believed was half an inch to three-quarters of an inch in diameter or width, could be something like a poker, chisel, spanner or tyre lever. There was a possibility that the same instrument could have been used to break into the flat. The assailant's clothes would have been bloodstained and neighbours in the vicinity of the murder scene were asked to search their dustbins for anything suspicious. Council dustmen were also asked to keep a lookout when they made their collections. In the midst of the horror, there was a touch of black humour. Forensic experts were called to nearby flats where occupiers had found a trail of blood on their communal stairway. Tests revealed it was not human blood. The culprit had been a neighbour's cat and its victim a bird.

In the first few days of the investigation, appeals were made for anyone who may have seen a man leaving No. 13 or spotted a car in the area, in the early hours of Friday the 14th. A milkman, on his way to work, reported having seen a man, who was described as being between 5 feet 5 inches and 5 feet 8 inches tall, of stocky build, with dark tidy hair and a heavy moustache, leave the front door of the tenement at 4.30 a.m. He was wearing faded jeans and a dark jacket. Police later issued his photofit picture. Police also wanted to trace the movement of a dark green Mini Countryman estate in the vicinity of Allan Street or on the Aberdeen–Stonehaven road, or adjoining roads, or in Stonehaven itself, between the times of 9.30 p.m. on Thursday 13 July and 6 a.m. the following day. Cabbies and long-distance lorry drivers were urged to pass on any information.

A couple, who were collected by taxi from the Treetops Hotel and dropped at the junction of Allan Street and Irvine Place between 12.30 and 1 a.m. on 14 July, never came forward.

The search for the murder weapon stretched beyond the city boundary. A squad of fifty uniformed policemen drew curious glances as they combed ditches and fields along both sides of the sixteen-mile-long Aberdeen–Stonehaven road. Verges along the main railway line to the south were also checked. A metal-detector was used to comb a beach at Stonehaven while officers checked a blowhole on the cliffs at Crawton, south of the town, which had been used as a rubbish tip. In Stonehaven, two policemen accompanied binmen on their rounds. Household and hotel refuse was checked. Police divers searched parts of the River Dee and were on call to probe the dangerous waters round the Kincardineshire coast.

It was four days after the killing when the fact that Dr Page occasionally worked for an escort agency became public. The police had established that she had been at home until 8.45 p.m. on Thursday the 13th, that she had later dined with the two businessmen at the Treetops Hotel and that she had driven herself home alone before she had met her death sometime during the early hours of Friday morning. The businessmen were quickly eliminated from police inquiries. The media played up the victim's 'double life'. It had been claimed that Dr Page's family and colleagues had no clue of her secret. She may have been discreet with clients about her background but she certainly told her family about her escort work. Adams, the cover name she used while carrying out escort duties, was her mother's maiden name. Dr Page and her mother, Mrs Florence Page, who died in 1993, often joked about her spare-time activity. She told her mother that the work only involved going out to dinner and that some of people she met had been really nice.

During a press briefing, Detective Chief Inspector Ritchie said it was only fair to point out that there had been nothing improper in her activities. Her last evening out had been purely social and completely above board. The women on the agency's books were mainly teachers, students and professional women during the day who were able to hold bright, intelligent conversation with clients. Apparently, Dr Page had persuaded a colleague to join the agency but she had later changed her mind. But Dr Page obviously enjoyed the occasional night out at a top restaurant with good food and good company. Her elder sister, Mrs Rita Ling, believed that she was lonely. It was as simple as that.

A week after the apparently motiveless killing, Mr Ritchie revealed that there was a strong possibility her attacker may have been known to her. He also said, 'There were signs of a struggle and there is a possibility that her assailant was scratched.' In making this disclosure, police hoped it would quell public anxiety that a killer was on the loose.

During the weekend of 21–23 July, the hunt for the elusive murder weapon spread from Aberdeen to Edinburgh. In the Granite City, people, who had travelled on the 6.25 a.m. Aberdeen–Edinburgh train on the day of the killing, were being interviewed. In the capital, a special incident centre was set up and two detectives from the Grampian force supervised the search by uniformed officers from Lothian and Borders. They were looking for a green duffel bag, which may have held the weapon, along with bloodstained clothing, shoes and a watch. However, the police were reluctant to say how they knew of existence of this bag.

A tracker dog helped in the search which covered the area around Waverley Station and the university. They also scoured the Grassmarket, a cobbled space in the Old Town, where public executions once took place and a mob lynched Captain Porteous of the City Guard in 1736. Police also visited lodging houses in Edinburgh in case the bag had been found by a dosser. The canvas bag was perhaps the key to the mystery. Detective Chief Inspector Ritchie said at the time, 'If we were to find this bag, we would be in a very strong position to make an arrest.' But, despite the exhaustive search, there were no new leads.

The funeral of Dr Page took place in the parish church of Rushmere St Andrew in the Suffolk countryside, near Ipswich, on 27 July. Among the thirty-one wreaths and floral tributes was one from her shattered colleagues at Aberdeen University whose message read, 'We are unable to express adequately our sadness.' Two of the university's staff attended the funeral. Dr Page's mother, Florence, broke down at the graveside and she and the rest of the family never got over their loss. Mrs Page's ashes are buried in her daughter's grave.

At the time of her death, Dr Page had been looking forward to going on holiday to the Isle of Wight with elder sister, Rita, and Rita's family of three sons. The plan was that Brenda would drive there with her mum but sadly, this was not to be.

Dr Page had been a pupil at Northgate Grammar School in Ipswich before graduating with a BSc degree from the University of London. She later obtained her PhD at the University of Glasgow. She was appointed to the post of cyto-geneticist at the University of Aberdeen in 1973. At the time of her death, she held the post of principal cyto-geneticist in the university's genetics department. Aberdeen's oil boom was taking off and she carried out groundbreaking research on the dangers facing divers in the North Sea.

She was academically gifted and she was also very creative. She could paint, crochet, knit and cook superbly. She made her own bridal dress for her wedding to biochemist Dr Christopher

Harrisson at St Mary-le-Tower Church in Ipswich in May 1972. She just seemed to excel in everything she touched. She also loved sport. Dr Page's father, Victor, was a keen sportsman. He had always wanted a son and both his daughters were brought up playing sports. The girls had played tennis together and Dr Page was also a very good swimmer. She also loved animals and, in her student days, she had taken home a brood of chicks that had been reared in the lab, during an embryo experiment, rather than dispose of them.

Dr Page had moved into the Allan Street flat that she shared with her three cats after her marriage had failed in 1975. In a brief statement issued by Aberdeen solicitor David M Burnside, Dr Harrisson expressed his 'sincere and heartfelt grief at the tragic and untimely death of [my] former wife' and said that he hoped the person or persons responsible would soon be apprehended. He also added that he had cooperated fully with the police and had been able to give them a detailed account of his movements around the time of her murder. Dr Page's cats were later adopted by one of her university colleagues.

In 1996, ex-Detective Chief Inspector Ritchie returned to Allan Street for the first time since the murder. He told *Evening Express* journalist Gordon Argo of his intense frustration at the outcome of the case, which had involved his team working some days round the clock. During the first week of the inquiry thirty-five detectives had been involved. In spite of tremendous support from the public, identification parades and the circulation of 5,000 posters through-out the city, the police still couldn't trace the killer. Mr Ritchie, who had retired from the force in 1984, said, 'What sticks most in my mind was that we were never able to place anyone at the scene of the crime.'

Allan Street has changed little since the murder although on-street parking in the area is more of a problem than it was in 1978. To combat this, the wooden garden fence at No. 13 has been removed to provide additional parking for cars.

23

BLACK FRIDAY

1981

On 12 September 1644, a blood-red moon hung in the night sky above Aberdeen. Next day, 13 September 1644, was truly an unlucky Black Friday for its citizens when the much larger Scottish Parliamentary Army that had been defending the town was defeated by a Royalist force led by James Graham, Marquis of Montrose, who had commanded the Covenanters at the Battle of the Brig o' Dee in 1639. What followed was a public relations disaster for Montrose. His troops, comprising of Irish and Highlanders, sacked Aberdeen and 118 townsfolk were slain in the rout. Wealthy citizens were stripped to preserve their clothes before being butchered. Montrose's reputation was blackened. The Battle of Justice Mills was fought amid the cornfields, valleys, slopes and burns in the area of the upper Hardgate, the ancient highway to the Bridge of Dee and the south. The Covenanter artillery was located on a steep hill overlooking a wide, green glen, now greatly reduced by modern development.

Let the clock tick forward more than three centuries to another Friday – 23 October 1981 – when John Alexander McLean (51), a casual labourer, was seen drinking in two city-centre pubs, The Grill and the Star and Garter. Before midnight, he bought chips at the Crossroads fish bar, at the corner of Crown Street and Springbank Terrace. But, not long after he had left the premises, something upset him and he began shouting at one or more persons. Six hours later, housewife Doris Robertson (61) was exercising her dog, Max, when she came across Mr McLean's body

175

at the place where Montrose's wild Gaels had once charged. Mrs Robertson, whose flat overlooked the murder scene, saw what, at first, she thought was another dog. Max, sensing danger, backed off. The body was lying curled up on the ground but she didn't touch it. Only when the milkman joined her did she realise that the man was lifeless.

Police with tracker dogs and serious-crime detectives were soon at the scene in Willowbank Road. Chief Superintendent George Souden told reporters at an on-the-spot interview at the incident caravan, 'We are treating the case as murder and are looking for the public to come forward if they saw this man last night. We are also looking for information regarding his movements after closing time.' Yards away a white plastic tent shielded the body. It had been found at the edge of grassland, popular with dog-walkers and joggers. As Mr Souden spoke, about fifty policemen carried out house-to-house inquiries in a district that today is still characterised by its a large number of guest houses. They also spoke to drivers who had parked in the nearby overnight lorry park.

Next day, police revealed that McLean had sustained severe head injuries as a result of a savage beating. As a country lad from Pitcaple in Aberdeenshire, he had moved to the city in his twenties. He had become a loner who slept rough and he was believed to have been attacked while he was making his way towards derelict property where he would spend the night. Murder posters were put up in the hope that detectives would solve the mystery of the dead man's last movements. They pulled out all the stops in their quest for witnesses but the site where the body was found is close to the bustling night life in the city centre and tracing people who had attended functions and parties in the area on the night of the murder didn't prove easy. Taxi drivers were also contacted. Detectives wanted to know what had caused the apparent row between the small, bearded man and the person or persons unknown. Was this linked to the incident?

Within a few days, police discovered a vital clue – personal property belonging to the deceased was found stuffed down a drain in nearby Bon-Accord Street. The find seemed to support one theory – that he had been the victim of a mugging. Chief Superintendent Souden said, 'It is possible he may have been robbed but it is unlikely he had a lot of money on him.' The night McLean died, he was wearing a blue parka, jeans and leather cowboy boots. So could he have been mistaken for an oil worker? In reality, the chances were that the attackers had more money on them than their poor victim. City bikers were contacted to see if they could help the police trace two motor cyclists who had been seen in the area. Several motorists were also sought. The police investigation did reveal that two youths had been spotted near the victim when he had stopped halfway along Springbank Terrace. He was leaning against a dyke finishing off his chips.

Seven weeks after the murder inquiry opened, the police received an important lead. Two youths, fitting the descriptions of the above-mentioned duo, had been seen peeking round a corner as McLean had made his way unsteadily along Springbank Terrace. The police believed these lurking youths had been the killers ready to pounce on their helpless prey. In the middle of December 1981, they issued a photofit picture of a baby-faced youth who they believed was one of the two who had been spotted in the area. His companion was a dark-haired youth wearing a dark leather jacket. But, after that, the trail ran cold. The baby-faced youth and his pal were never traced – and the brutal murder of a lonely, harmless man remains unsolved.

The year 1981 proved frustrating for Grampian Police. On 18 June, the body of sub-postmistress Dorothy Park (63) was found bound and gagged in her flat behind the village post office at New Pitsligo, Aberdeenshire. Her callous killers fled with a meagre £79, leaving the kindly spinster struggling for breath on the kitchen floor. The inept killers had overlooked £4500 of pension cash which was lying on the living room sofa. Miss Park's body was found next morning when the local newsagent called with the morning paper. Two strangers, both in their twenties, seen acting suspiciously outside the post office on the night of the murder, and an off-white 1100 or 1300 car, later spotted speeding from the village, have never been traced.

24

FINAL FARE

1983

On Saturday 22 October 1983, thousands of fans arrived at Aberdeen Football Club's home ground unaware that they were potential suspects in a murder mystery. The secret operation was mounted by police in a bid to trap the killer of Aberdeen taxi driver George Murdoch (58) who was found dying, with head and neck wounds, beside his cab in a quiet city suburb. Three weeks after the murder, police had learned that their chief suspect, dripping blood from an injured hand, had visited a chip shop barely a mile from the crime scene. His thumb and first three fingers of his right hand were cut. They played a hunch that the wounds might still be visible. So, as 22,800 spectators filed into Pittodrie Stadium to watch the Aberdeen–Celtic Premier League match, police officers were waiting at each of the forty-four turnstiles serving the terracing and stands.

More than seventy-five officers had orders to stop and check the hands of every male, aged between sixteen and thirty, but many more people were only too willing to cooperate. Fans with gloves were asked to take them off. Supporters did not know what was happening until they were inside the ground. Detective Superintendent Jim McLeod, who was in charge of the inquiry, later told reporters, 'We never realised there would be so many people with cuts.' Although a massive number of people were checked, the match kicked off on time. Police were delighted with the cooperation they received from the fans. They didn't get a single complaint – which said a lot for the way in which the

179

officers had carried out their task. Over the weekend, the murder-inquiry team started checking the details of those fans who had had cut hands. But, unfortunately, the operation threw up no fresh leads. (A further appeal for information was made at Pittodrie before the Aberdeen–Dundee Scottish League Cup tie on 5 October.)

The murder of George Murdoch led to one of the city's most relentless manhunts. It had begun on the busy evening of Thursday 29 September after Murdoch, who worked for City Taxis, picked up his fatal last fare in the city's West End. At 8.03 p.m., he had picked up a fare from Aberdeen University's Central Refectory in Old Aberdeen and had dropped his passenger at the top of Queen's Road, near Angusfield Avenue. At 8.26 p.m. and heading back into town, he reported, 'Clear at Do' School [the old School of Domestic Science].' Base told him to come nearer to town. At 8.28 p.m., he was midway through his shift when he called his controller from slightly further down Queen's Road to say he had a 'pick-up for Culter'.

Fifteen minutes later in dimly lit Pitfodels Station Road, two teenage cyclists saw the taxi driver in a life-and-death struggle with his mystery passenger. They saw that the attacker had Mr Murdoch pinned to the ground and that he was strangling him. The cyclists sped off to call the police from a phone box on North Deeside Road. Passers-by found the cab driver's body beside his sky-blue Ford Cortina which was parked near the top of Pitfodels Station Road, a steep brae that runs from North Deeside Road south to Garthdee Road. The driver's door and a rear passenger door were open. The killer had ransacked the vehicle for money before fleeing with the dead man's wallet and some cash.

One of the passers-by used the cab's radio and contacted City Taxis' controller to say that there was something wrong with their driver. One local man at the scene at first thought that there had been a hit-and-run accident. The taxi firm dispatched two cars to Pitfodels but, by time they arrived, an ambulance and the police were already there. Detectives found a cheese-cutting wire, with wooden handles, at the scene and this was believed to have been in the wanted man's possession. The cheese-cutting wire was described as 'valuable evidence' and, although detectives do not believe it was used to kill George Murdoch, it has been kept in case it ever becomes possible to produced it in court.

The detectives had a description of the man involved in the death struggle. He was aged between twenty and thirty, about 5 foot 7 inches tall, of thin build, with short dark hair and clean shaven. He was wearing dark clothing – possibly a dark, round-necked jersey and dark trousers. It seemed likely his clothing would have been bloodstained. A motorist came forward the next day to say that, at 9.05 p.m., she had seen a 'white-faced' man, fitting that description, running along North Deeside Road towards the city, 300 yards from the murder scene. He was described as looking 'frightened'. Joggers were known to be in the vicinity around the same time but Detective Superintendent McLeod believed that the frightened man was going too fast to be a jogger and that he was actually fleeing the murder scene.

The next day, 30 September, roadblocks were set up on South Deeside Road, on the opposite side of the river from Pitfodels, after a man was reported acting suspiciously in the vicinity of Storybook Glen, the small theme park for young children, at Maryculter. Tracker dogs joined the hunt but this man was never traced.

Six days after the killing, the police announced a vital new lead. A Ford Cortina taxi, possibly the victim's, picked up a scruffily-dressed man from a hotel in Queen's Road on the night of the murder. It was either the New Marcliffe or Belvidere. It transpired that the man, who was very drunk, had been turned away by a barmaid at the New Marcliffe. He was asked to leave the hotel bar at around 8 p.m. on the Thursday night and he did so without causing trouble. Police believed that the man may have gone from there to the nearby Belvidere before getting into the taxi. His description closely fitted that of the main suspect. Two bus drivers and a taxi driver confirmed that the taxi was double-parked in Queen's Road, facing out of town, towards Hazlehead, and that a man was getting into it. A young couple, who were passengers in a taxi that was seen overtaking Murdoch's taxi as his fare got in, were never traced.

The local media pulled out all the stops to give Grampian Police maximum coverage of the crime. Reporter Alison Shaw and photographer Jim Love of the *Evening Express* flew over the West End in a light aircraft. They were accompanied by Detective Sergeant Alec Den, who pointed out the route George Murdoch would have driven with his final fare. At the controls of the four-seater plane was Peter Forbes of the Pegasus Flying Club. Meantime, a team of sixty policemen was working round the clock to try to nail the killer. It meant a fourteen-hour day for detectives and uniformed officers alike. Detective Inspector Warren Souden, the younger brother of Chief Superintendent George Souden who was mentioned in the previous chapter, summed up the relentless routine thus, 'When I came home last night the wife and kids were all in bed asleep. When I came out this morning, they were still sleeping. But that's the job.'

There were many unanswered questions facing detectives. George Murdoch had told his controller his pick-up was going to Culter so why had he turned off North Deeside Road into Pitfodels Station Road? North Deeside Road would have taken him directly to his fare's suburban destination. Did his killer force him to turn off the main road on to this deserted road? Was the killer the frightened man spotted running towards the city? Or did he escape along the path of the old Deeside railway track, either going east and crossing the river via the Bridge of Dee or, perhaps, heading west to the bridge at Maryculter? Either route would have taken him on to the South Deeside Road and away from the city. Soon after the murder, police had searched surrounding woodland and thick undergrowth in the belief that possibly the killer had holed up after his dark deed. Even farmers were requested to search their land.

But soon a note of disappointment was sounded by police. Despite repeated appeals to the public in the press and on radio and TV, they were becoming frustrated by the lack of response from key witnesses. George Murdoch's grief-stricken family had also made an impassioned plea to the public to come forward, if they had any information, and reward money, offered by individuals in a bid to catch his killer, amounted to £1600.

On the eve of George Murdoch's funeral at Grove Cemetery, Woodside, the *Evening Express* published 1000 posters in the hope that they would stir the memory of anyone who could help. The posters depicted his taxi double-parked on Queen's Road as he was picking up his fatal fare. Both the police and the newspaper helped distribute the posters to shops, pubs and bookies. But, as potential witnesses hesitated in coming forward, the police appeared to have got their strongest lead.

An incredible three weeks after the murder, they learned that a young man, dishevelled and sweating, had been served in Mr Chips fish and chip shop on Great Western Road in Mannofield. Witnesses particularly remembered him because of the blood that had been dripping from a hand injury on to the counter. He had also had scratches on his cheek and nose and there was the beginnings of a bruise on the lower lid of one of his eyes. Staff and a customer reported that he had come into the chip shop about fifteen minutes after the cyclists had seen George Murdoch struggling for his life. And their description of him was similar to that of the police's main suspect. He was aged between nineteen and twenty-five, 5 foot 8 inches to 5 foot 11 inches tall, slim, with short brown hair and he was clean shaven. He was wearing a dark jersey and trousers and a black leather jacket and he had an Aberdeen accent. To all intents and purposes, it was an enhanced description of the killer.

As well as the shop manager and the girl assistant who had

served him, there had been about six customers in the chip shop at the time. Detective Superintendent McLeod told the media that, during the five minutes the man had been waiting to be served, a man behind him made a jocular remark to him – possibly about his appearance. Detectives were astonished that no one in the shop had connected the dishevelled customer to the killing about a mile away. 'How we have not heard about this before I just can't understand,' commented the baffled senior detective. He disclosed the vital lead had been revealed to police during door-to-door inquiries in Mannofield.

However, yet again, police were to be frustrated. Of the six customers who had been queuing in the chip shop that night, only one was ever traced. It was a bitter blow. One or perhaps two of the customers were believed to have been playing squash at nearby courts. Up to twenty potential witnesses chose silence rather than coming forward. One frustrated officer was heard to say, about reluctant witnesses, 'You wouldn't believe it but we are having to find these people ourselves and go to them and ask what they saw or did not see.' But police efforts never flagged. Indeed the investigation was still going strong a year later. Every home in Culter, the killer's supposed destination, was visited and door-to-door checks were carried out in the West End of Aberdeen. Detectives collected, studied and filed more than 6000 statements and, for the first time in an Aberdeen murder hunt, a computer was used to gather information. At police headquarters today, there are twenty-four volumes of evidence still on file.

Jim McLeod, who first walked the beat with the former Aberdeen City Police Force in 1956, held the rank of Detective Chief Superintendent when he retired as boss of Grampian Police CID in March 1988. Although the force did everything possible to solve the crime, failing to crack the Murdoch murder was a bitter disappointment for McLeod. He believed, and still believes, that the prime suspect may not have realised he had committed a murder. He probably thought he had committed an assault and robbery, which might explain why he entered Mr Chips soon after the murder, his hand dripping blood and most likely sharing that joke with another customer.

His victim, George Murdoch, who lived in Mastrick, left behind a widow. The couple had been married for thirty-seven years and George had been working as a cabbie for eighteen months. It seemed he enjoyed his job although he was not too keen on working the late shift. His brother, Jim, a former taxi driver, was well aware of the potential dangers of job and he had suggested a 'panic button' be installed in cabs. And Jim McLeod has never given up hope that the killer will face justice. The wanted man, he suspects, probably has a criminal record. If he is still alive, he would be aged between forty and fifty at the time of writing. Meanwhile, detectives might one day nail the killer by means of DNA fingerprinting. The taxi-driver murder is one of the 'cold' cases on which they have focused their recent inquiries.

MURDER AND THE PARANORMAL

In 2000, Dr Peter McCue, a member of the Scottish Society for Psychical Research, received a letter from an Aberdeen man who had experienced a possible case of precognition – the ability to be aware of future events – regarding the Murdoch murder. Mr Brian Parry (not his real name) switched on his car radio one morning in 1983 and 'heard' details of the murder. He mentioned the report to two colleagues but they said they hadn't heard of or read about the incident. The mystery deepened when Mr Parry could find no mention of the crime in his paper that evening. But, five weeks from the day of the elusive 'news bulletin', Aberdeen awoke to details of George Murdoch's murder, exactly as Mr Parry had predicted.

Six months after writing to Dr McCue, Brian Parry, who was then in his sixties, received a visit from two detectives. They gave him George Murdoch's cloth cap and pen and asked him to handle the objects in the hope he could give them a lead. Mr Parry informed Dr McCue, 'I could not help them in that respect but I said that they would not get the killer, in my opinion.' (In parapsychology, the supposed ability to deduce facts about events by touching objects related to them is known as 'psychometry'.) Dr McCue, a consultant clinical psychologist in Glasgow, wrote to Mr Parry's two former colleagues. Only one replied but he couldn't recall whether the murder was mentioned before or after the incident. Mr Parry's wife said that her husband had definitely told her of his experience *prior* to the murder.

Dr McCue's account of the case was published in the September 2001 edition of *The PSI Report*, the newsletter of the Scottish Society for Psychical Research.

SOURCES

Adams, Norman, *Scotland's Chronicles of Blood* (Robert Hale, 1996).

Argo, Gordon, 'Unsolved Murders from Grampian Police Files', *Evening Express*, 16 November, 1996.

Brogden, W A, *Aberdeen: An Illustrated Architectural Guide* (Rutland Press, 1998).

Campbell, Jack, *A Word for Scotland* (Luath, 1998).

Harris, Paul, *The Garvie Trial: The Crime that Shocked Scotland* (Impulse, 1969).

Hopkin, Archibald, *The Aberdeen Pub Companion* (Retro, 1975).

Irvine, Hamish, *The Diced Cap: The Story of Aberdeen City Police* (Aberdeen City Corporation, 1972).

Knox, Bill, *Court of Murder: Famous Trials at Glasgow High Court* (John Long, 1968).

McCue, Peter, 'Two Cases of Possible Precognition', *The PSI Report*, September 2001.

Marren, Peter, *Grampian Battlefields* (Aberdeen University Press, 1990).

Piper, Peter, 'Who Killed the Waterfront Waif?', *Scottish Sunday Express*, 16 October 1955.

Roughead, William, *Knaves' Looking Glass* (Cassel & Co, 1935).

Smith, Sir Sydney, *Mostly Murder* (Harrap, 1959).

Stockman, Rocky, *The Hangman's Diary: A Calendar of Judicial Hangings* (Headline, 1993).

Whittington-Egan, Richard, *William Roughead's Chronicles of Murder* (Lochar, 1991). Wilson, John, (Editor) 'The Trial of Jeannie Donald', in *Notable British Trials* (William Hodge, 1953).

Wilson, Richard, *Scotland's Unsolved Mysteries of the Twentieth Century* (Robert Hale, 1989).

Young, Alex F, *The Encyclopaedia of Scottish Executions* (1750 to 1963) (Eric Dobby, 1998).

In course of his research, the author also consulted the following publications:

Aberdeen Evening Express, Aberdeen Free Press, Aberdeen Journal, Daily Record, The Glasgow Herald, The Herald, People's Journal, The Press and Journal, Scottish Daily Express, Scottish Daily Mail, Scottish Sunday Express.

INDEX

INDEX

190

INDEX

INDEX

192